THE *Blue Peter*
GREEN
BOOK

Lewis Bronze, Nick Heathcote and Peter Brown

BBC Books/Sainsbury's

THE BLUE PETER GREEN BOOK . . .
. . . is printed on paper produced by Papyrus Nymölla, an
environmentally-friendly paper mill. The paper pulp is non-chlorine
bleached so that cancer-causing dioxins, once associated with the
process, are not produced. The mill uses carefully managed
forests and recovers 97% of all chemicals used.

THE AUTHORS
This book has been written by three members of the
Blue Peter production team – Lewis Bronze, the editor;
Nick Heathcote, a former *Blue Peter* producer, now in
charge of *Newsround*, and the person who thought up
the idea of the Green *Blue Peter* Badge; and Peter
Brown, a *Blue Peter* film director, who has produced
many of the programme's environmental items, and
who created the *Blue Peter* Wildlife Garden.

Published by BBC Books,
a division of BBC Enterprises Limited,
Woodlands, 80 Wood Lane, London W12 0TT
First published 1990
Reprinted 1990 (three times)
© Lewis Bronze, Nick Heathcote and Peter Brown 1990
© Foreword by Lord Sainsbury 1990
ISBN 0 563 20886 4

BBC Books would like to thank Friends of the Earth
for their advice on many of the topics;
Greenpeace for their advice on pages 42–3 and 44–5;
British Nuclear Fuels for their advice on pages 38–9.

Book design by Neville Graham
Typeset in 10/10½ Plantin Light by Ace Filmsetting Ltd, Frome, Somerset
Printed and bound in Great Britain by Butler & Tanner Ltd, Frome, Somerset
Colour separations by Dot Gradations Ltd, Chelmsford
Cover printed by Lawrence Allen Ltd, Weston-super-Mare

Contents

About this book 4
Going Green 6
A delicate balance 8
The food factory 10
The root of it all 12
Riches of the rainforest 14
Eating the rainforest 16
The Greenhouse Effect 18
Wealth from waste 20
Natural art 22
Living under a cloud 24
Turning your pet Green! 26
Countryside in the city 28
A man-made wilderness 30
Drive into the future 32
Energy for life 34
Acid rain: the big rot 36
The nuclear debate! 38
Down with CFCs! 40
Feeling like a swim? 42
Sealife in danger 44
A day at the coast 46
Going fishing? 48
Animals matter 50
Back from the brink 52
Beauty and the beasts 54
The Green Shopper 56
Graffiti's Here, OK? 58
Taking action 60
The Green *Blue Peter* Badge 62
Finding the facts 63
Index 64

About this book...

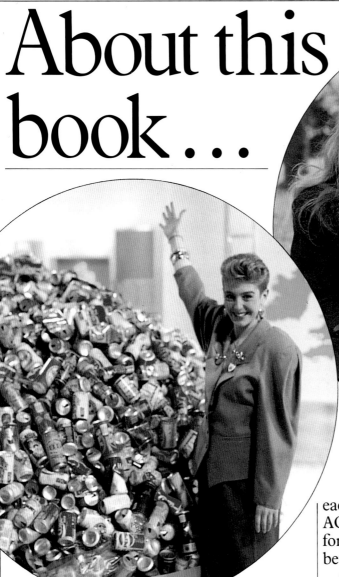

Caron finding out from Andy Goldsworthy how to turn nature into art! (See pages 22–3.)

Yvette launching *Blue Peter*'s aluminium can recycling campaign. (See pages 20–1.)

THE THEME OF THIS BOOK is hope. It is the hope that, as the children of today grow up, they will want to live in a cleaner and kinder world, a world that is not choking itself on filthy smoke, nor using up precious supplies of fuels, nor polluting its rivers, seas and countryside with poisonous rubbish.

In this book, the main threats to our planet are explained clearly. Knowing what the problems are is only the first step – the next is doing something about them. On each double-page spread, you will find an ACTION BOX which gives you some ideas for things you can do now, ideas to make a better world.

On *Blue Peter*, we know that hundreds of thousands of children in Britain were very concerned about their surroundings and wildlife long before the word 'green' became fashionable. We know that many of the 'environment-friendly' products now available were bought in the first place because children alerted parents to the dangers of the old type of products. We know that children can make a real difference to their surroundings, through cleaning up litter, creating wildlife gardens, joining in recycling schemes and many other ways. It is hard for poor old adults to change their ways, and start using cars less, or remember to drop glass off at the bottle bank. But children can get them to do it!

4

John makes sure Bonnie is kept on a lead as requested in this London park. (See pages 26–7.)

KEEP YOUR
ON A LEAD

I WAS DELIGHTED to be asked to write this foreword because I have admired *Blue Peter* for a long time and used to watch the programme with my own children. I particularly like *Blue Peter* because it sets such high standards – something that we at Sainsbury's also try to do. The programme is especially good at explaining interesting and important subjects in an entertaining and enjoyable way. One of its aims, I know, is to help all who watch *Blue Peter* realise how much we need to protect the world we live in.

Nowadays, many people are worried that we are not taking care of our planet. Scientists tell us that unless we find a way of solving some of the problems that the human race has created over many years, the earth – our environment – will suffer even more. No-one wants that, which is why the first step should be to help everyone understand the problems.

We all have a part to play – we can't just leave it to the experts. At Sainsbury's we are trying to contribute in many different ways, by building and running our supermarkets so that they do not damage the environment and by selling products which are more friendly to it.

I am sure *The Blue Peter Green Book* will be tremendously important in encouraging young people to get things done; Sainsbury's is proud to be sponsoring it.

Thousands of people have already won their Green *Blue Peter* Badges, for the work they are doing to protect our planet. Find out how to win yours on pages 62–3.

Children are the future. You can make sure that what has been called the 'green bubble' does not burst. You are not burdened by the habits of a lifetime, as adults are. Children are the voters, workers, bosses and government of tomorrow. Start making your voice heard now.

Lewis Bronze, Editor *Blue Peter*

Lord Sainsbury of Preston Candover

Going Green

MAKE NO MISTAKE, it's a war! Each side in the battle to save our planet has its own weapons. On this page are some of the villains, like dirty factories, polluted air and chopped down rainforests. On the opposite page are some of the many ways we can help clean up the planet.

Humans have been living on this planet for two million years, but it is only in the last couple of hundred that we really have made a mess of it. Before it is too late, people have to change their ways. We have to stop using up precious things that can never be replaced, and we have to stop ruining the land, sea and air.

Left: Smoking chimneys and car exhaust pipes are pumping tons of rubbish into the air all the time – and we breathe it in. (See pages 18–19, 24–5 and 32–3.)

The rainforests contain a huge variety of animals, insects, birds and plants. So why does Man seem determined to wipe them out? (See pages 14–17.)

Right: Polluting gases fall as acid rain. Large forests and thousands of lakes have been ruined already. How can it be stopped? (See pages 36–7.)

Cheap, clean and safe ... sometimes. This explosion in the Soviet Union shows it can go terrifyingly wrong. Should we have more nuclear power – or none at all? (See pages 38–9.)

Ivory looks best on elephants, but tusks are valuable and many elephants have been massacred. They are being wiped out in parts of Africa. (See pages 50–1.)

ACTION–How you can help

This is a battle everyone can fight. By joining groups that campaign to protect the environment, by taking the action suggested in this book, by getting your family and friends interested, you can make a difference to the future.

'Going Green' is complicated. Britain cannot go back to the days before there were factories or fertilisers, cars or chemicals. 'Greener', cleaner things like electricity made from wind power will never give us all we need. We have to find a balance between the good and the bad, and we have to try and make the bad better. We hope this book will help you make up your mind about some of the difficult questions and choices we face.

Left: Don't throw away bottles and drinks cans! Save newspapers! It saves energy if they are recycled – and cuts down on rubbish! (See pages 20-1.)
Right: Millions of cars now run on lead-free fuel. That is only the first step to cleaning up the muck cars belch into the air. (See pages 32-3.)

RECYCLING

LEAD-FREE

ALTERNATIVE ENERGY

ENDANGERED SPECIES

The osprey, our most spectacular bird of prey, was brought back from the brink of extinction in Britain. Find out how creatures can be saved. (See pages 52-3.)

FREE-RANGE

Electricity does not have to come from power stations that burn coal or oil. Will we ever turn our lights on thanks to the wind? (See pages 36-7.)

Which hens are allowed to peck and strut, and which are cooped up in cages? Find out how to be a Green Shopper. (See pages 56-7.)

A delicate balance

MAN CREATES HABITATS as well as destroying them. Some of the best are man-made – like hedgerows. There are 300 000 miles of hedge in Britain and each provides a haven for thousands of wild animals and plants. Hedges are important because they attract insects and act as 'wildlife motorways' for foxes and badgers. Most hedges were made in the eighteenth and nineteenth centuries when a change in the law allowed farmers to enclose their fields, though some hedges, used as parish boundaries, are known to be over 1000 years old. We must protect our local hedgerows – with pesticides driving animals away from the countryside and habitats being destroyed, hedges are important sanctuaries for wildlife.

Vanishing hedgerows

Britain's patchwork of hedges (above left) is disappearing at the rate of 4000 miles a year to create huge, featureless prairies like this one in Sussex (above right).

IN FIELDS divided by hedges farmers can waste a lot of time turning their tractors, so in areas with enormous fields of crops, like East Anglia, hedges are being removed. Over the last 45 years a quarter of our hedgerows have been destroyed to create large 'prairies'. Without hedges, winds can erode away the topsoil, so the Government is now encouraging farmers to look after hedgerows.

How old is a hedge?

A ROUGH WAY to tell the age of a hedge is to count the number of species of woody trees and shrubs in a 30-metre stretch. One new species gets established about every 100 years, so a hedge with five species would be 500 years old. However, some recent hedges have been planted with mixed species, so it's a good idea to check old maps to make sure the hedge has been there for some time. The older the hedge, the more important it is to protect it.

Trees and shrubs

Hawthorn makes an ideal foundation for a hedge because it is fast-growing and sturdy. Its thick and thorny branches are good for enclosing farm animals and it makes a good home for wildlife. Other hedgerow trees include hazel, blackthorn, rowan, and silver birch. Buckthorn provides a good nesting site for birds and they feed on its black fruits in autumn.

Blackbird

Oak

Hazel

Blackthorn

Bracken

Butterflies

The appearance of the orange-tip butterfly at the end of April is one of the first signs that summer is on the way. However, only the male has orange wing-tips. The caterpillars feed on hedgerow plants such as cuckoo flower, garlic-mustard and lady's smock. The red admiral and small tortoiseshell butterflies lay eggs on stinging nettles, which provide shelter and food for their caterpillars.

Hogweed

Red admiral on stinging nettle

Garlic-mustard

Plants

Garlic-mustard is a member of the cabbage family and grows in colonies in the shade of hedges. The leaves smell of garlic when you crush them. Butterflies, such as the orange-tip and green-veined white, lay their eggs on the flowers. Other hedge plants such as dandelions, ground ivy and stinging nettles provide shelter for slugs, snails and beetles.

Birds

Hedges provide food and nesting sites for birds including blue tits, blackbirds and robins. The song thrush is partial to snails which it finds under hedges. It holds the snail in its beak and smashes it on a rock (a 'thrush anvil') until the shell shatters. The wren is a tiny bird which darts in and out of hedges searching for insects and spiders.

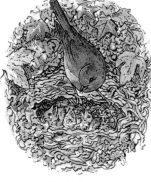

Robin feeding young

A hidden world

A HEDGE is like the edge of a woodland. Under it grow shade-loving plants and climbers, such as brambles and briars, which provide food and shelter for insects. Most hedgerow plants need insects for pollination and insects, in turn, attract predatory birds and small mammals. In a mature hedge the whole system has reached a delicate balance where each species relies on the presence of others for survival.

Typical food chain

| Leaf | Caterpillar | Beetle | Shrew | Fox |

Hawthorn

Elder

Peacock

Hornbeam

Holly

Dandelion

Orange-tip

Mammals

Weasels are fierce predators and use hedges to stalk mice and other rodents. Hedgehogs and shrews forage along hedgerows sniffing out beetles, snails, slugs and worms. Hedgehogs can move very quickly, and can usually cover a mile during a night's hunting. In winter they hibernate under piles of dead leaves. Foxes use hedges as cover to reach their hunting grounds. Bats, such as the pipistrelle, swoop low over hedges in search of insects which they eat in flight.

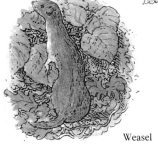

Weasel

The food factory

IN AN EFFORT to grow more crops to an acre of farmland, our countryside is fast becoming one big food factory drugged with chemicals. Out go the traditional farming methods like 'crop rotation' which have been used successfully for centuries. In come the chemists with artificial fertilisers and killer sprays, all at enormous cost to wildlife, the environment and, possibly, our health. Intensive farming now produces more food than farmers can sell. While chemicals are good for a quick reward, they are disastrous for the land in the years to come. Here's why . . .

The problem with pesticides

PESTICIDES are chemical poisons which farmers spray onto crops to kill off weeds and insect pests. Their effect on wildlife has been devastating because pesticides don't just kill off pests – they also poison animals which are harmless.

But, most disturbing of all, is that some pesticides remain in the food even when it reaches our supermarket shelves. Nobody knows the long-term effects of eating food contaminated with pesticides. Scientists suspect that some of the pesticides approved for use in Britain could be linked with allergies and types of cancer. Because nobody is certain the Government has now set limits for the amounts of pesticides allowed in some foods, but it's impossible to check that the rules are always followed.

Some vegetables are sprayed with pesticides (above) just to make them *look* more appetising – as many as 46 doses before they reach our supermarket shelves! Pesticide-free vegetables (below) vary in size and shape but are just as delicious! Those produced using traditional methods are said to be 'organically grown'.

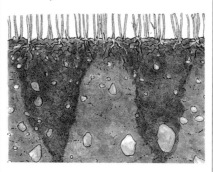

Nitrate fertilisers
Nitrate fertilisers are used to increase a farmer's crops and are made from fossil fuels so, like petrol and coal, one day they'll run out. Nitrates get washed away by rain into streams and rivers, causing the oxygen level to drop and killing off fish and other aquatic life. Drinking water in some areas now contains several times the agreed safety level of nitrates. Scientists fear that nitrates could be a cause of illness in bottlefed babies.

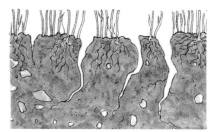

Soil erosion
If nothing is put back into the soil to replenish it, it will eventually lose its fertility. Farmers used to put manure on their land, which rots to form humus. Humus holds the soil together. Without it, heavy farm machinery and then rain can mean the topsoil is just washed away. This soil erosion is a serious problem throughout the world and it leaves the ground useless for growing crops.

Intensive farming
An aerial armada of chemicals is sprayed routinely onto the crops to turn this field into a food factory. An overdose of fertiliser is what makes crops grow while the soil becomes nothing more than an anchor for the roots.

The choices

GO ORGANIC! Organic farmers have been growing vegetables for years without using pesticides and using only natural fertilisers. They can't grow as much to the acre as intensive farmers, but their methods are much better for the land in the long term. Organic farming can't, as yet, supply all our food needs so the answer probably lies somewhere between the two for the time being.

But we can all go organic in our own gardens and allotments.
1 Try mixed planting – growing onions and carrots together helps ward off the different pests.
2 Try to encourage nature's own pesticides into your garden.

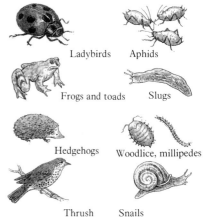

Animals to encourage | The pests they eat
Ladybirds | Aphids
Frogs and toads | Slugs
Hedgehogs | Woodlice, millipedes
Thrush | Snails

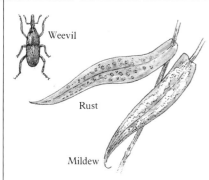

Weevil

Rust

Mildew

Pests and diseases
Pests such as weevils, aphids and fungi are poisoned by pesticides, but so are millions of butterflies, small mammals and birds. The pests themselves soon become resistant to pesticides so chemists have to keep developing new ones.

These frogs, which are beneficial to farmers because they eat pest insects, were turned bright orange and speckled by a hormone pesticide in a farmer's field – and they were the lucky ones!

The root of it all

A WALK THROUGH A wood is a walk through a kaleidoscope of shapes and colours: no two trees are the same and there is all the variety of glades of wildflowers. You never know what you are going to see next – maybe a glimpse of a woodpecker or a badger. Stop and listen and you'll hear birdsong. Even a lone oak tree is like a 'Noah's Ark' in the landscape – it has so many nooks and crannies that it is home for over 140 different types of insects!

Trees are vital for our survival because they provide food, shelter, medicines and even the air we breathe! Even so, over the last 40 years millions of trees have been destroyed.

How it used to be

A T ONE TIME most of Britain was covered in forest and our towns started out as clearings among the trees. There are still the remains of ancient woodland, but most of it has been lost under fields, factories, motorways and housing estates. When the large forests went, so did the beavers, wolves and bears which used to live wild in Britain. Badgers and foxes survived by keeping low when people came near. Some animals, such as red deer, survived because William the Conqueror ordered many woodlands to be designated Royal Forests to protect them for hunting. There were severe penalties for villagers who cut down trees or poached deer. Preserving trees as food and shelter for deer saved many of today's older trees from the peasant's axe.

Above: Many forests survive today because they once provided cover for stag hunting.
Right: An oak tree provides food and shelter for many mammals, birds and insects.

Conifers or broad-leaved trees?

MOST TREES planted in recent years are there to provide timber. Varieties of conifers were introduced from overseas because they are quick-growing and survive well on damp moorlands. However, they are usually planted in rows so close together that hardly any light reaches the forest floor, and so nothing grows among the pine needles. Attractive as they are, these forests are 'wildlife deserts'. What we need are more broad-leaved forests with trees such as oak, beech, ash and birch which make ideal habitats for wildlife.

This plantation of conifers in the Yorkshire Dales is almost devoid of wildlife. Couldn't we grow broad-leaved trees instead?

Destruction of trees

THE 'Great Gale' of October 1987 was the worst natural disaster to hit the south-east of England for over 250 years. Thousands of trees were destroyed and the homes of hundreds of people were damaged.

But for the trees it wasn't all bad – after the storm, people woke up to how important trees are in towns and the countryside. They realised how much they missed a particular tree or line of trees and wanted to take action. We can all do something to help trees by following the ideas in the Action Box.

We think of trees as permanent features in the landscape. It's only after they are destroyed by gales that we realise how much we miss them.

ACTION

● **_Look after_** old trees in your area by giving them a bucket of water in dry weather.
● **_If you think_** someone is about to chop down a tree, contact the Tree Officer at your District or County council.
● **_Create_** a tree nursery and grow trees from seeds to transplant into parks and gardens. Collect seeds in the autumn. Some seeds, such as oak, hawthorn and birch, need cold weather to come to life. Bury them outside in a jar of sand over winter. (The jar will protect them from squirrels.) In spring, prepare the nursery by removing weeds and raking over the soil until it is fine. Dig up your seeds and plant them. When the trees are about 1 m high transplant them to their final sites.

Water your seedlings regularly.

Riches of the rainforest

THINK OF ALADDIN'S CAVE, full of chests brimming with multicoloured jewels, riches beyond your wildest dreams. . . . To someone who studies plants or insects, animals or birds, the tropical rainforests of the world are one big Aladdin's Cave. Nowhere else is there such a rich mixture of life, nowhere else contains so many secrets we have yet to discover, secrets that might cure illnesses or prevent disease, or perhaps provide new sources of food.

With so much to offer, it is an international disaster that the rainforests are being 'eaten up' at such an alarming rate. Whether it is Central and South America, Africa, or countries like the Philippines and Malaysia in the Far East, the story is the same. Rainforests are being destroyed to make way for 'civilised' man, to grow crops, to provide timber, to 'develop' the land. About half the world's rainforest has already gone. An area the size of England, Scotland and Wales goes up in smoke every year.

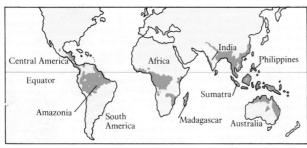

Where are the rainforests?
They are scattered in a broad band across the Equator. They range from the forests bordering the Great Barrier Reef in Australia to the forests of Central America. The largest is mighty Amazonia – over five million square miles. But it's being eaten away by logging, land clearance for ranching and farming, mining, damming, and new roads. In Madagascar, just a ribbon of forest is left along the eastern coast and that too is endangered.

Rainforest life

WE ARE LOSING SPECIES at an astonishing rate because of the destruction of the rainforests. About 50 a day, or one every half hour or so, disappears off the face of the earth forever. Each one plays some part in the balance of nature in the rainforest. And while species are disappearing, we might be losing forever cures for crippling diseases.

Rainforest people
There are thought to be about 200 million tribal people living in the rainforests – that's nearly as many people as live in America. The tribal peoples might lack our modern, 'advanced' knowledge, but they know how to harvest the rainforests, which plants can be eaten, and which ones are medicines. From Borneo to Brazil, their lands are in danger.

Indian from Brazil

Flowers and plants
Thanks to a little rosy periwinkle found in Madagascar, nearly all children now recover from the blood disease, leukaemia. Rainforest plants are like a chemist's counter and thousands of them contain things that are or can be used in medicines. Beautiful rare orchids are traded, but they belong in the tropics as much as ivory belongs to an elephant.

Rosy periwinkle
from Madagascar

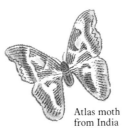

Atlas moth
from India

Macaw from
South America

Animals and birds
The thick layers of vegetation between the forest floor and the treetops provide a choice of habitats for the teeming wildlife of the rainforests. Most creatures live in the canopy, just below the treetops. Some exotic animals – like the komodo dragon and the huge atlas moth – are unique to the rainforest. Some are very rare and endangered, like the lemurs of Madagascar and the mountain gorillas of Rwanda. About half of all the species in the world live in rainforests.

Mountain gorilla
from Rwanda

Tropical rainforests support thousands of species of animals, insects and plants.

ACTION

The rainforests are far away, but you *can* help to save them.

● *Never* let your family buy anything made out of tropical wood – large pieces of furniture, a garden bench, even a salad bowl. Do not buy anything made out of teak or mahogany – if you do, you are asking loggers to cut down more trees.

● *Make sure* the wood you buy is pine, oak, beech or ash. These are not tropical woods, and can be replaced.

● *Check* that orchids at the garden centre are home-grown.

● *If* you want a parrot as a pet, make sure it is hatched in Britain. If the bird is ringed, it was probably hatched here. Tell the pet shops you will not buy imported parrots.

● Friends of the Earth run a Tropical Rainforest Campaign. Their address is on page 63.

How trees breathe

RAINFORESTS play a big part in regulating the world's climate and atmosphere. The broad-leaved trees of the rainforests absorb carbon dioxide from the air and release oxygen. With fewer rainforests, less carbon dioxide is being absorbed. More carbon dioxide means that more heat from the sun will stay locked up in our atmosphere – and that could be devastating. (See pages 18–19.)

Strangely enough, given the life and vitality of a healthy rainforest, the soil in the forests is very poor. What makes the rainforest thrive is the particular combination of trees and soil. Once the trees are gone, the soil is not good enough to grow crops.

This scene of total devastation is of rainforest in the Amazonian region of South America. The area originally looked like the picture on the left!

Eating the rainforest

HAMBURGER, CHEESEBURGER, chilliburger, quarter-pounder . . . yummy! We love them, and we buy millions from fast food restaurants every year. They're cheap, they're very quick, they taste good, and they don't even do you much harm. But when you chomp into a burger, do you ever stop to think about how that burger has reached you? The simple truth is, your favourite fast food snack could be doing more damage to the planet than just about anything else you come into daily contact with.

Fast food started in America, just over 30 years ago. In those days, most of the meat for the burgers came from cattle farms in Central American countries like Costa Rica. The trouble was, and is, that the land in those countries is not really suitable for beef farming. First, large areas of rainforest have to be chopped down to provide grazing land for cattle. With the trees gone, the soil soon loses its nutrients, and after a few years, it becomes useless for grazing cattle. It's wasted. The forest cannot be replaced and the cattle farmer has to go somewhere else, to begin the destruction again. Since the late 1950s, most of the rainforest in Central America has been lost this way, and a huge area in the Amazon forest in Brazil as well.

Below left: Devastated rainforest in the Amazonian region of South America.

Left: Rainforests in Central and South America are often cleared to grow food, such as soya bean, for European cattle.

Food for thought – meat

In Britain, most burgers – and probably all the burgers made by the bigger fast food chains – come from cattle bred in Britain or Europe. But unfortunately, your burger might still be helping to destroy rainforests. Here's how: the cattle are fed on food that makes them grow quickly, like soya bean, and most of that comes from Brazil, where enormous forests have been cleared to make fields for growing soya.

Food for thought – french fries

The potatoes that have been turned into your french fries are probably the only part of your fast food meal grown here in Britain. But they'll come already smothered in salt, which nobody really needs. Too much salt in your food can turn into a health hazard as you get older. Don't forget about the bag the french fries come in – that was once a tree, although some chains now use recycled paper for their bags.

Packaging problem

NOT ONLY is your burger probably helping to destroy the rainforest, the carton it comes in is also doing long-term damage to our poor planet. It is possible that the carton is polystyrene 'blown' with chlorofluorocarbons – CFCs – that are destroying the ozone layer. Some big companies have stopped using CFCs, but even so, what have you got? A plastic container that you might use for a minute but which will take centuries to decompose. Or it might be burned in an incinerator, possibly giving off harmful gases into the atmosphere. And before they get to the dump or the incinerator, many burger cartons spend a long time littering our streets as some people are too lazy to find a rubbish bin. Whatever happened to fish and chips wrapped up in newspaper? It's a healthier meal, it doesn't destroy rainforests, and although the newspaper was once a tree, it has a second life wrapped around a piece of cod.

ACTION

● *Ask* where the meat in your burger has come from. More importantly, ask what the cattle were fed on, and where *that* came from.

● *Ask* for healthier food. Some companies now do veggie burgers, or beanburgers. Try them. Try baked potato fast food snacks. Growing potatoes does not destroy rainforests.

● *Complain* about the unnecessary packaging they give you in fast food restaurants.

● *Do not* litter the streets with your fast food containers.

● *If* you eat a lot of burgers – say, more than two trips to a fast food place a week – try and eat different types of food.

The Greenhouse

CITIES OVERFLOWING with sea water, coastal areas washed away, fertile farmlands turned into barren dustbowls, storms and hurricanes common even in Britain . . .

It sounds like a horror film but it's what the world could be like in less than fifty years from now. Because we are misusing our planet, we are making it hotter, through what is called the greenhouse effect.

As the world gets hotter, there will be more droughts in Africa and America, leading to food shortages. A slight rise in the yearly average temperatures means the polar icecaps will begin to melt. *That* will raise sea-levels, causing flooding in low-lying countries like Bangladesh. All over the world, the weather will be more violent, with an increase in typhoons, hurricanes and storms.

There's no doubt about the causes of the climatic changes. *It's up to us to do what we can to stop them.*

What is it?

UP IN THE ATMOSPHERE, energy, in the form of light from the sun, streams towards earth. It passes through layers of gases miles above the surface of the earth. As the sun warms the land and sea, energy is reflected *back* at these gases. But this energy is not in the form of sunlight – it is invisible infra-red energy, which the gases absorb. They trap this heat, and that's where the term 'greenhouse effect' comes from. It's as if the whole planet is roasting inside a greenhouse. If the greenhouse effect did not exist at all, the earth would be a frozen, lifeless planet, but at the moment it is building up much too fast. The main 'greenhouse gases' are **carbon dioxide**, **methane** and **CFCs**.

Electricity
Most of the electricity we use is produced by the burning of fossil fuels – coal, oil and gas. When these are burnt, they give off carbon dioxide. So, whenever you turn any electrical appliance on – hi-fi, light bulb, TV, or washing machine – think 'Do I really need to use this?' And don't forget to turn it *off*!

Cars
Cars add to the greenhouse effect because they have carbon dioxide and nitrogen oxide in their exhaust fumes. The fuel crisis of the mid-1970s forced car makers to produce cars that went further on a gallon of petrol, but we are still wasting precious petrol and putting yet more CO_2 into the atmosphere on pointless car journeys.

Right: This picture shows what is happening to our world. It's as if we are living in a greenhouse.

A rise in temperature will mean more polar ice melting (above). Sea-levels are already rising 1 mm each year, and that could increase to 10 mm a year. Cities like London and New York might be flooded (left). It will cost billions of pounds to build sea walls to protect Britain's east coast. Fertile, low-lying farmland might be lost forever.

Cows
Cattle produce methane and as more people need more cows to provide them with milk and meat, then more methane will be produced. It is the same problem as the rice fields – we have to have the food, so we must suffer having the methane too. If more people became vegetarians, we might manage with fewer cows.

Effect

Heat reflected back into the atmosphere

Heat from the sun

Heat trapped by 'greenhouse gases'

CFCs
Chlorofluorocarbons are well known for the damage they are doing to the ozone layer (see p. 40). They are a double attack on our planet because they are also 'greenhouse gases'. Aerosols, foam plastic fast-food containers, padding from cushions and cars, coolants from fridges and air conditioners all contain CFCs.

Rainforests
Destroying rainforests (see pages 16–17) has awful consequences. This is adding to the greenhouse effect in *two* major ways. Trees need carbon to grow. They get it from carbon dioxide (or CO_2), and forests absorb millions of tons of it a year. Cut the trees down, and the amount of CO_2 eaten up is also cut. To make matters worse, most of the wood is burnt. That *releases* millions of tons of CO_2 which add to the greenhouse effect.

Rice
Methane is also produced when vegetation rots underwater. That is what happens in the millions of square miles of rice fields all over Asia. As the world's population increases, more rice will need to be grown, releasing yet more methane. It is increasing in the atmosphere at an even faster rate than carbon dioxide.

Rubbish
Most household rubbish gets buried in landfill dumps. Just because it is out of sight, does not mean it does no harm. Methane is released into the air as the rubbish rots. It is the most effective greenhouse gas – one molecule of it absorbs twenty times as much heat as one molecule of carbon dioxide.

The sea
The sea absorbs vast quantities of carbon dioxide, which is good. To keep soaking it up at the same rate, the amount of salt in the water should not fall. But water that comes from melting polar ice has no salt in it. It will absorb less carbon dioxide. As the greenhouse effect gets worse, the sea will help us less.

ACTION
We must act now if we are to slow down the greenhouse effect and *you* can do something!
- *Never* waste electricity.
- *Cut down* on pointless journeys made by car. Keep a diary of the number of times your family car is used in a week. Suggest that several journeys could be combined into one trip, saving petrol.
- *Use* public transport more, if it is available. Or, ride a bicycle or walk instead. You'll get fit too!
- *Recycle* as much waste as you can. (See pages 20–1.)
- *Write* to your Member of Parliament. Ask: 'What are *you* doing to stop the greenhouse effect?' *We* must make them understand it is very serious and countries *must* act together to stop it.

Wealth from waste

PEOPLE USED TO describe Britain as 'an island built on coal, surrounded by fish'. These days, Britain is more like an island built on rubbish, surrounded by pollution. Every year, each household in Britain creates about 1 tonne of rubbish that has to be thrown away. If it *wasn't* taken away, the streets of our towns would be impassable rubbish mountains. But much of our rubbish is not rubbish at all! Most of it could be recycled.

What happens to our rubbish?

ONCE THE dustmen have taken rubbish away, most of it gets dumped in huge landfill sites. Most sites eventually get covered with soil, but they cannot be used to grow crops, and they are not strong enough for buildings. Meanwhile, all the rubbish inside them begins to decompose and all kinds of nasty, poisonous things seep down into the soil. Many of them seep into the water supply. Fires on landfill sites are common because of chemical reactions taking place below the surface. Other rubbish is burned in incinerators – but sometimes that releases toxic fumes and leaves poisonous ash behind.

Most household rubbish gets buried in vast underground mountains, but putting it out of sight is not the answer.

Why recycle?

RECYCLING MAKES SUCH perfect sense, it is amazing people are not forced to do it by law! When something is recycled it saves on finding fresh raw materials to make the same item. Most importantly, it also cuts down the amount of energy needed to make that item. It takes less heat to make a glass bottle out of broken, recycled glass than it does starting afresh with the raw ingredients. Less heat means using less oil or coal.

How to recycle

THE KEY TO successful recycling is **sorting**. Recycling is more efficient if different types of items are separated into categories – the more, the better. Rubbish can be split up into paper, glass, metal, organic waste (food, dead flowers, potato peelings, tea leaves etc.), plastic and things made out of a mixture of items. At the bottle bank, glass can be separated again, into brown, green and clear. By using magnets, metal cans can be separated into steel and aluminium (aluminium will **not** stick to a magnet).

What can be recycled?

PAPER
Paper is made from trees. Each year, everyone in Britain gets through six trees' worth of paper. Making new paper harms the environment as the process usually involves chlorine bleach, which pollutes rivers. It's far better to use unbleached, recycled paper. Not only can newspapers be recycled, but also magazines, cardboard, paper bags and envelopes.

GLASS
Most high streets now have bottle banks. Remove all tops first, then recycle drinks bottles, jam jars and sauce bottles. *But never recycle bottles that can be reused* like milk bottles. It's more efficient to refill them with milk than to recycle them to make new bottles. If glass is not reused, it lasts forever, broken and buried in the soil.

ORGANIC MATTER
If you have a garden, you need never again throw away vegetable peelings, uneaten or rotten food. Get an old dustbin, drill a few holes in it, and pop off to the fishing shop. Buy some brandlings – worms that will happily munch away on your rubbish. In a few months you will have lovely black compost to put on the garden.

METAL
Most cans are made out of steel. As steel is magnetic, you can throw it

Blue Peter's BabyLife Appeal was the biggest aluminium can recycling scheme ever launched.

out and it will be magnetically separated out and recycled at a waste centre. If aluminium cans are not recycled, it is a great waste of the energy it takes to make them. As they are not magnetic you need to separate them out of your rubbish.

CLOTHES
Yes, you can recycle old clothes! Take them along to charity shops like Oxfam. Some will be sold, others will go to the Oxfam Wastesaver Unit in Huddersfield. That is where the thousands of tons sent in by *Blue Peter* viewers in the 1987 Rags Appeal went. Clothes are sorted according to material and returned to textile mills for recycling.

ACTION

● *Sort out* your rubbish. Good recycling only begins when things are separated out from each other.
● *Find out* where your nearest bottle banks, can banks and wastepaper skips are. Use them.
● *Write to* your local council to get them to provide these skips and banks if your area does not have them.
● *Avoid* plastic wherever you can. It's very difficult to recycle.
● *Use* recycled paper.
● *Run* local litter-picks, and recycle cans and bottles.
● *Raise* money for local environmental projects, by selling aluminium cans to scrap metal dealers.

Natural art

W HAT CAN YOU DO with a pile of fallen leaves? Andy Goldsworthy makes them into the most beautiful sculptures! Andy is a 'land artist' and his sculptures are made entirely out of natural materials which he collects without harming the environment. He has worked with stone, petals, feathers, tree trunks and even ice and snow. Some of his sculptures are designed to last a long time – others melt or rot away, so the only record of them is a photograph. Andy's ability to surprise makes people look at the environment in a different way.

'Holes are very inviting', says Andy, 'and make you want to peer into them.' That's true whether it's a hole in a pile of leaves (right) or an ice hole at the North Pole (below).

This patch of horse chestnut leaves was made by tearing similar-sized red and yellow leaves and sticking them together.

This curious horn is a continuous spiral of sweet chestnut leaves. Each leaf is laid in the fold of the next leaf and stitched together with thorns.

The 'leaf streak' (above) explores the colours in horse chestnut and was made by tearing sections from yellow leaves and sticking them to green leaves using thorns.

Andy created this 'dandelion hole' (left) from newly flowered dandelions at a sheltered spot on a grass verge near Bretton.

ACTION

● **_The great thing_** about natural materials is that they don't cost anything. Create your own sculptures using leaves, rocks or other materials and explore ways of combining colours and textures. Avoid harming the environment and use only materials which are plentiful.

Living under

WE ALL MAKE AN impact on the environment through our daily lives and the only way to protect our planet is to adjust our lifestyles so *we* become more 'environment-friendly'.

Think of the ways you, as an individual, can help. Try to use only 'renewable' resources, such as food grown in a way that does not damage the land for the future. Rely less on fossil fuels by cutting down on the amount of electricity you use at home. Think of ways of reducing the amount of rubbish you throw away by recycling more and avoiding wasteful packaging.

If enough people act in a small way it will make a world of difference to the future.

Right: This picture shows an imaginary urban area 'before' and 'after' environmental improvements.

Make your town better!

EVEN SMALL changes to urban surroundings can mean big improvements for the people who live there. Two views of the same area are shown below: the top one *before* and the bottom one *after* a number of improvements have been made to the environment. Look at *your* local area and think of ways you could make it better for people and wildlife. You could even join or form an action group to campaign for changes. Local councils are usually keen to support well thought-out community schemes.

Rubbish
Rubbish dumped on wasteground is a danger to people and animals. Broken bottles and food cans cause injury to children and some household waste can spread disease.

Traffic
Traffic in many side streets is appalling. In parts of London the average speed of traffic is slower than a horse and cart! Think of the air pollution and danger to pedestrians.

Concrete jungle
Treeless, concrete deserts with the occasional container of foreign shrubs are uninteresting to the eye and encourage vandalism. People like to see nature around them which is why they keep window boxes and gardens.

Buses and bikes
Lift-sharing schemes cut down traffic. Bus lanes make travel by bus quicker than by car and this reduces the number of cars on the road. Cycle lanes encourage people to travel by bike – the cleanest form of transport.

Nature in towns
Wildlife gardens bring all the colour and variety of the countryside into the city. Urban woodlands break up the stark outlines of buildings and absorb dust from traffic.

a cloud

Graffiti and vandalism
Long, featureless expanses of concrete encourage graffiti (see pages 58–9) which gives the place an uncared-for feel. This, in turn, leads to vandalism and dumping.

Community art
Community-made murals and sculptures brighten up the landscape and show that people care about their surroundings.

Recycling
Community 'bottle banks' and 'newspaper banks' encourage people to separate reusable rubbish so it can be recycled.
(See pages 20–1.)

A Green home

THE GREENHOUSE EFFECT starts right here in our own homes. Our washing machines, tumble-driers, freezers and dishwashers all contribute to the greenhouse effect because they use electricity produced by burning fossil fuels (see pages 18–19). Saving electricity not only saves money, it cuts down on pollution.

Most energy in our homes is used for heating and cooling, and most of that energy goes to waste. A boiler with a badly adjusted thermostat can waste an enormous amount of heat. Heat also escapes through doors and windows.

Furniture
Avoid furniture made from hard-woods such as mahogany and teak. Most of this wood comes from the tropical rainforests of Indonesia and Malaysia (see pages 14–15). Softwoods are just as good for most purposes.

Heat
Stop heat being lost by fitting draught excluders to doors and windows. Keep doors closed. Double-glazing reduces the amount of heat lost through windows.

Household cleaners
Use 'environment-friendly' household cleaners. Use vinegar as a natural toilet cleaner and lemon juice to clean brass and copper. Use only 'phosphate-free' washing powders. Never put paint strippers or white spirit down the sink. Your local Council tip will dispose of them for you.

Recycling
Separate household refuse into glass, paper, metal and organic waste. Organic waste can be made into compost. Glass, paper and metals can be recycled. Plastics are a problem to dispose of – avoid them if possible.

ACTION
- *Think* of ways to make your home use energy more efficiently.
- *Campaign* to have bus lanes and cycle lanes in your area. Start a lift-sharing scheme.
- *Start* a local waste recycling scheme.
- *Plant* an urban woodland or wildlife garden to brighten up the city (see pages 28–9).

Below: Six ways to make your house more 'environment-friendly'.

Electricity
Save electricity by fitting 'energy-efficient' light bulbs. When your family is choosing washing machines and freezers, find out how much electricity they use.

Natural materials
Use natural materials around the home, rather than plastics. Tar paper on the roof is just as waterproof as plastic.

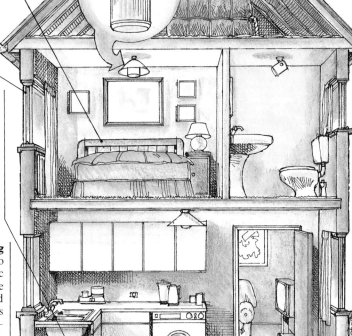

Turning your pet Green!

PETS ARE FUN! If you have ever had a dog or cat, you will know how much love and happiness they can bring into a home. Owning and caring for a pet has always involved a lot of responsibility to keep the pet healthy and happy. But owning a pet means more than that – it also demands responsibility towards your surroundings, towards other animals, and towards other people.

That is why pets are in *The Blue Peter Green Book*. Just like recycling or campaigning, a pet can be cared for in a way that helps the environment. The hard work is well worth it!

Neutering

OUR CAT, Willow, was neutered in 1989. Neutering means that a dog or cat cannot become a mother or a father. We had the operation done because we were shocked to discover the figures for unwanted kittens. The RSPCA alone destroys nearly *20 000* kittens every year – all of them cute and fluffy, but all unwanted and unloved.

Neutering makes sense for many reasons. It will stop unwanted animals being born. It will also make a dog or cat much more pleasant to live with. The natural urges of animals cannot be fully satisfied when they are household pets. They often become bad-tempered and aggressive. A female cat or dog on heat attracts every male in the area.

All the old wives' tales about neutering are not true. Neutered animals do not become fat, unless they get fed too much and do not get enough exercise.

A vet can tell you all about neutering. It is a simple operation and does not cost very much – certainly far less than looking after unwanted puppies and kittens. The only sign of Willow's operation was a shaved patch of fur which soon grew back. Ever since her operation she has been a much friendlier cat.

Willow was none the worse after her operation and became more friendly.

Unless cats are neutered, the number that are abandoned and have to be destroyed will keep going up.

Tracking dogs

A FEW YEARS AGO, the old dog licence was abolished. It was pointless, and cost the Government more to collect than it raised. Now there's a campaign for *dog registration* – a new way of keeping track of dogs.

The idea is to cut down on stray dogs and to trace owners of dogs which are running wild. Instead of simply buying a licence to own a dog, the new system would register each and every dog. It would cost money, but that could be spent on having dog wardens to round up strays. Every dog would be marked – either with a small tattoo, or by an electronic chip implanted just under the skin.

The RSPCA strongly supports dog registration. It could be just what's needed to win over people who dislike dogs and accuse them of all kinds of trouble. Bad owners would be rooted out and punished. The good ones would benefit from all the better publicity about dogs.

have you trained your Human yet!

Henry and Cleo say
'Keep Our City Clean'

Rochester Upon Medway City Council

A cartoon leaflet to teach people about dog mess. Many councils run schemes like this one.

Clean up after your dog!

DOG MESS is not only ugly – it can be dangerous too. If you have a dog, it is up to you to make sure it does not foul parks and pavements.

The main health threat caused by dog mess is through a little bug called *Toxocara canis*. The people most at risk from it are young children who might play in parks where dogs are allowed to roam. If they catch *Toxocara canis*, they might go blind or suffer brain damage. Nobody wants that, and no responsible dog owner wants to be accused of spreading disease and mess. More parks now have 'dogs only' and 'no dogs' areas, to give dogs a place to go and to keep some areas dog mess-free.

WARNING
Dogs' excrement has caused blindness in children. Please do not allow your dog to foul this green.
Abinger Parish Council

Top: Make sure your dog is trained properly!
Above: Many towns have 'dog-free' areas. People can be fined if they disobey the rules and let their dogs into them.
Left: Bonnie is not allowed to roam when children are near.

ACTION

- **_Get your vet_** to neuter your dog or cat.
- **_Clean up_** after your dog. Get a pooper-scoop!
- **_Find out_** where the 'dog-only' places are in your town. Ring the council.
- **_Use_** special 'dog-only' areas. Stay out of 'no-dog' places.
- **_Find out_** about dog registration. The RSPCA will send you details. (Their address is on page 63.)

Countryside in

A POOL TEEMING with strange animals and a marsh where insects are devoured by carnivorous plants! Not in the jungles of South America but on a rooftop at the BBC Television Centre in Shepherd's Bush!

The *Blue Peter* Wildlife Garden was originally a narrow strip of wasteland running over the roof of a pumphouse. In 1987 David Bellamy helped transform it into a haven for wildlife. Today wildlife refuges in built-up areas are more important than ever. If hedgerows are 'wildlife motorways', gardens are 'stepping stones'!

You too can help save Britain's vanishing wildlife by creating a wildlife garden.

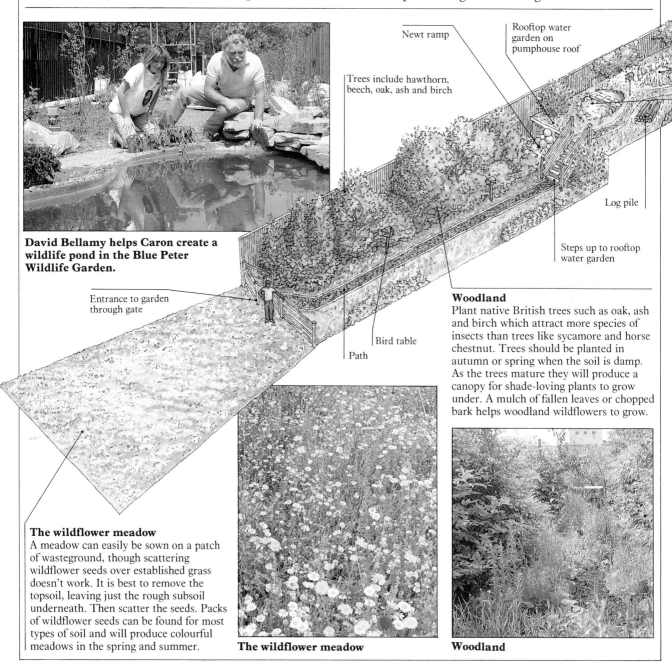

David Bellamy helps Caron create a wildlife pond in the Blue Peter Wildlife Garden.

Newt ramp

Rooftop water garden on pumphouse roof

Trees include hawthorn, beech, oak, ash and birch

Log pile

Steps up to rooftop water garden

Entrance to garden through gate

Bird table

Path

Woodland
Plant native British trees such as oak, ash and birch which attract more species of insects than trees like sycamore and horse chestnut. Trees should be planted in autumn or spring when the soil is damp. As the trees mature they will produce a canopy for shade-loving plants to grow under. A mulch of fallen leaves or chopped bark helps woodland wildflowers to grow.

The wildflower meadow
A meadow can easily be sown on a patch of wasteground, though scattering wildflower seeds over established grass doesn't work. It is best to remove the topsoil, leaving just the rough subsoil underneath. Then scatter the seeds. Packs of wildflower seeds can be found for most types of soil and will produce colourful meadows in the spring and summer.

The wildflower meadow

Woodland

the city

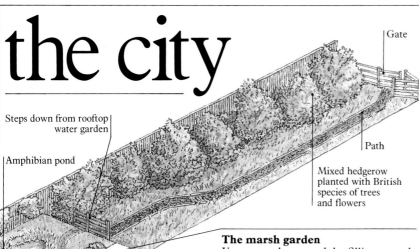

Gate

Steps down from rooftop water garden

Amphibian pond

Path

Mixed hedgerow planted with British species of trees and flowers

The marsh garden

You can make a marsh by filling a pond-liner with soil and sedge peat, then topping it up with water. Try planting a selection from: marsh marigold, water forget-me-not, flowering rush, water mint, brooklime, flag iris, bog bean, water plantain and sedge. Add rotting wood or rocks to make hiding places for frogs and newts. Marsh gardens can dry out quickly so they need watering regularly.

The pond

A pond attracts a wide variety of wild creatures. The ideal pool provides a range of homes: it should have shallow edges and shelves for insect larvae and tadpoles; a deep part for newts and diving beetles, and plants such as Elodea which keeps the water oxygenated. A bucket of water and mud from another pond will introduce thousands of tiny creatures to a new pond, but avoid fish – they eat all the interesting creatures! Birds use the edges of ponds to drink and bathe, and larger creatures such as foxes may visit at night and leave tell-tale footprints in the mud!

The pond

The marsh garden

How to make a mini-bog!

Several types of insect-eating plants can be grown outside in Britain. Sundews and butterworts grow wild in the peat bogs of Britain and Ireland and will survive outside all year round. Venus flytraps and pitcher plants come from warmer climates so they need to be taken indoors in the winter.

The easiest way to make a mini-bog is to grow the plants in a container, such as an old sink or baby's bath, filled with moss peat. Some insect-eating plants need to be watered with rainwater.

Bog plants are *very scarce* so should never be taken out of the wild. The Carnivorous Plant Society (see page 63) can advise you on where to buy insect-eating plants and how to look after them.

Your do-it-yourself mini-bog: sundew, butterwort and pitcher plants growing in an old sink.

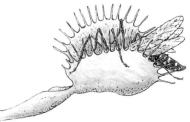

A Venus flytrap plant catching an unsuspecting insect.

Feeding the birds during winter

Every winter children from the Bentworth Primary School 'Bird Patrol' visit the *Blue Peter* Wildlife Garden to feed the birds and study them. Most of their hanging feeders are home-made from empty yoghurt pots and milk cartons. They fill them with peanuts to attract blue tits, great tits and greenfinches, and scatter kitchen scraps, fat and 'wild bird mix' on the bird table to attract black-birds, starlings, thrushes and robins.

The Bird Patrol hang home-made feeders on the bird table.

ACTION

● *Find* an area of wasteground and use the ideas on this page to create your own wildlife garden.

A man-made

T O A MIGRATING BIRD Sandwell Valley is like a green oasis among the concrete housing estates four miles from the centre of Birmingham. Forge Lake, in the middle of the valley, is flanked by the busy M5/M6 motorway junction, a polluted river, and a railway line. It is the last place you'd expect to find rare birds, but in 1988 birdwatchers spotted 135 species ranging from cormorants to woodpeckers, making it one of the RSPB's top ten bird reserves. What's astonishing is that every bit of the Sandwell Valley is man-made!

Right: Some of the birds you might spot if you visit the Sandwell Valley Nature Centre.

Canada goose

Lapwing

Common tern

Grey heron

Reed warbler

Fieldfare

Coalmines once tunnelled under Sandwell Valley, though the pits are long gone and the spoil heaps have merged into the landscape. Over the years, the marshes caused by subsidence became a refuge for birds. So, when the water authority wanted to flood part of the valley, the RSPB said, 'why not design a lake that will make a bird reserve?' and that's what they did. The picture above shows the work in progress. Above right shows Sandwell Valley and the Nature Centre today.

Left: Sandwell Valley is a green oasis only four miles from the bustling centre of Birmingham.

wilderness

Spotted crake

Sparrowhawk

Redshank

Greenshank

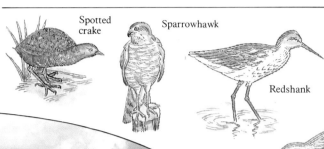

The 'Wader Scrape' was scraped out of mud to create a shallow pool for wading birds to paddle about in search of worms and small creatures. Visitors can watch seabirds like Greenshank and Redshank 100 miles inland!

Little ringed plover

Jack snipe

Great crested grebe

Turnstone

Hides have been built alongside the lake and wader scrape so that visitors can get really close to the birds without scaring them. The footpaths and wheel-chair ramps leading into the hides are hidden by grassy banks and bushes.

Man-made islands were created in the lake to attract nesting birds. Willow branches anchored down with poles provide leaf cover for great crested grebe and protect their eggs from crows.

Right: Sandwell Valley Nature Centre has over 30 000 visitors a year. The centre is most valuable to local children who use it for nature studies. Here they are showing David Bellamy the centre's wildlife garden.

ACTION

- **_Look_** for derelict sites in your area which could be made into wildlife reserves.
- **_Ask_** the landowner if you can photograph and record animals and plants living there.
- **_Think_** of ways to make the site more attractive to wildlife.
- **_Discuss_** your ideas with the local wildlife trust or branch of the RSPB who can help you put them into action.

Drive into the future

B Y THE END OF 1989, one in three of all Britain's motorists were filling up with unleaded petrol. That figure is a stunning victory for the people who tried to get Britain to convert to lead-free at the start of the 1980s. For months, they had to put up with the government, the car makers, and the petrol companies saying 'there's no proof lead does any harm'. The truth is the opposite. Lead added to petrol to make cars run better *does* affect the brain – especially the growing brains of children. In 1981, the Government declared lead-free petrol would not be introduced. Eventually they changed their minds.

Since the autumn of 1989, *all* new cars have to run on unleaded petrol. Congratulations to the campaigners of CLEAR (the Campaign for Lead-Free Air) who are fighting the battle to take harmful lead out of the air we all breathe.

Cars are dirty

T HE FUMES THAT COME OUT of a car's exhaust are dirty, smelly, and can harm both the air and people who breathe them in.

In the days before unleaded petrol, the fumes contained small amounts of the metal lead, which came out of the exhaust as tiny particles of dust. Lead is poisonous to people. It is not just a question of breathing in the fumes – if the dust gets on food we eat, or onto books and desks we work with, we can breathe it in.

Unfortunately, lead is not the only nasty ingredient in car exhausts. Both carbon monoxide and nitrogen oxide also pollute the air.

Anyone who lives and works near lots of motor cars will probably absorb more lead into their bodies than someone who does not. Many schools in big cities are near motorways or busy road junctions, where traffic might be stationary for ages with engines running.

Catalytic converters

The polluting gases can be removed by catalytic converters. These go inside the exhaust system and remove carbon monoxide, nitrogen oxide and hydrocarbons. They only work with unleaded petrol. But even catalytic converters have their problems. First, they're expensive, although some car makers fit them for no extra charge. Second, they give off carbon dioxide, one of the main greenhouse gases (see pages 18–19).

How a catalytic converter works

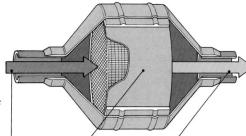

Exhaust fumes from engine going in.

This is where carbon monoxide, nitrogen oxide, and hydrocarbons are absorbed.

Exhaust fumes coming out with pollutants reduced but still with carbon dioxide.

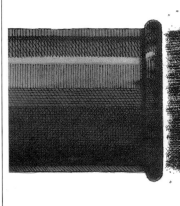

Blue Peter goes lead-free

Letitia Luff with Caron as the first of Letitia's winning posters is pasted up in the centre of London.

IN 1989, *BLUE PETER* ran a competition to draw attention to Lead-Free Petrol Week, run by CLEAR, which had the aim of making one big final push towards unleaded petrol.

The rules were to design a poster which would be shown on over 800 giant sites around the country during Lead-Free Petrol Week, and also used on thousands of smaller colour pictures. The winning entry was by Letitia Luff, who was ten at the time, and comes from Reading.

The poster marked the climax of the campaign against lead in petrol. In the seven years it lasted, the number of petrol stations selling lead-free increased from about zero to over half in the country – about 10 000. It is too early to be precise, but the amount of lead in the air should drop by about one-third, as it has done in the United States. *Blue Peter* is proud of its part in such a successful campaign.

John made sure that his car used unleaded petrol before he bought it.

The choices

EVEN LEAD-FREE PETROL harms the environment. The best long-term answer is to find a fuel which is cleaner and 'greener'.

Lots of other fuels have been tried. The milkfloat which delivers your pinta probably has an *electric* motor. But they cannot go far before they need to be charged up, and their batteries are very heavy.

Another answer might be fuels called **ethanol** and **methanol**, made out of plants, but they are very expensive.

Looking into the next century, there is the possibility of cars running on **hydrogen**. Another long-term hope is **solar** power, using energy from the sun to power car batteries. At present, these cars look funny and are just experiments – but they might eventually provide a replacement for cars using dirty, polluting, running-out petrol.

This solar-powered car may look strange alongside a bus, but solar power may drive cars in the future.

ACTION

● *Use* unleaded petrol. If your family car *could* be running on unleaded, make sure it is.
● *If* your family is buying a car, make sure it runs on unleaded.
● *New* cars could have catalytic converters – ask your family to choose a car with one. It need not cost any more.
● *Less* use of cars. Walk or cycle. Combine several car journeys into one longer drive. Using cars less saves fuel, which means less pollutant gases released into the atmosphere.

Energy for life

OUR MODERN, hi-tech world depends on energy to keep it going. A look around any town shows just how important energy is. We rely on it for lighting, heating, cooking, washing, transport and industry. We need it to power everything from televisions and computers to watches and pocket calculators. The list seems endless but supplies of many of the fuels we use certainly aren't and our energy needs are costing the environment dear. Coal, oil and gas are still our main sources of energy but they are all limited and will run out one day. There's nuclear power, too, but that has its drawbacks, so scientists are now looking at ways of harnessing the almost limitless supplies of natural power from our sun, winds and seas.

Coal, oil, gas

COAL, FIRST MINED in huge quantities in the eighteenth century, powered the Industrial Revolution. Today, it provides about a third of the world's energy and is one of the main fuels used in power stations to make electricity. Oil supplies almost half of *all* energy used. It powers cars, planes, ships and trains, fuels power stations and is the raw material for products like plastics and paints. Natural gas provides about a fifth of the world's energy and about a quarter of Britain's. Most of the UK's gas comes from the North Sea.

**Above: A modern coal mine in Yorkshire, England.
This natural gas platform (far left) is in the North Sea, and this oil refinery (left) is in Texas, USA.**

Limited energy

FOSSIL FUELS oil, gas and coal are 'non-renewable' energy resources. Once they've gone, that's it – and we're getting through them at a frightening speed. Scientists reckon that if we carry on using the reserves we *know* exist, at the present rate, then the world's oil will have run out by about 2030 and all natural gas will have been used by about 2045. There's probably enough coal to last until about 2240 but it can't fully replace oil or gas and it creates a great deal of pollution when it's burned.

WORLD FOSSIL FUEL RESERVES (Estimated 1989)
Oil – 920 billion barrels Runs out 2030
Gas – 110 trillion cubic metres Runs out 2045
Coal – 1020 billion tonnes Runs out 2240

Polluting the air

ACID RAIN is one of the worst types of pollution we're creating, but it's not new. A hundred years ago, Britain's first air pollution inspector, Robert Angus Smith, used the phrase to describe the polluted rain in Manchester. He reported that the city's air was not only filthy but also acidic and it was attacking vegetation, stone and ironwork. Amazingly, his report was forgotten until the 1960s. Then, Scandinavian scientists began to link pollution, blown across the sea from Britain and other European countries, with the high amounts of acid in lakes and rivers which were killing fish. Today, acid rain has spread around the world, destroying whole forests and their wildlife.

Power stations

Coal- and oil-fired power stations are the worst offenders when it comes to acid rain. Scientists reckon they produce most of the man-made sulphur dioxide that can turn into deadly sulphuric acid. But by 2003, with the help of new technology, the government plans to cut output of this gas from British power stations by 60% of the 1980 level.

ACTION

● **_Cut_** air pollution and save energy by using less of it, especially electricity!
● **_Switch_** off lights in unused rooms and don't waste hot water.
● **_Don't_** overheat buildings or leave windows open unnecessarily.
● **_Persuade_** people to insulate buildings, so heat doesn't escape.
● **_Walk_** or cycle instead of going in a car.
● **_Persuade_** people to fit catalytic converters to their cars. (See pages 32–3.)
● **_Join_** organisations concerned about the energy we use and the effects it has on our environment. (See page 63.)

A poisonous cocktail

Power stations which burn fossil fuels, industry and cars belch out a poisonous cocktail of polluting gases, including sulphur dioxide and nitrogen oxides. These combine with gases like hydrogen and oxygen to produce two destructive types of acid, sulphuric acid and nitric acid, which eventually fall to the ground, as acid rain, causing widespread damage.

Cars and lorries

In their exhaust gases, cars and lorries produce much of the nitrogen oxide that can turn into nitric acid, then acid rain. More and more cars can now have catalytic converters fitted to their exhaust systems to remove this polluting gas. (See pages 32–3.)

Acid rain: the big rot

ACID RAIN is literally eating away at our Earth, destroying woods, forests and even the historic buildings in our cities. It is also polluting our rivers, lakes and soil. But, it doesn't stop there. The toxic mixture of gases we produce and pump into the air can damage people's health and kill plants and animals by destruction of their habitats or pollution of their homes. Already, thousands of European and American lakes have been poisoned, killing most of the fish that lived there. Huge areas of forests have also died.

The root of it all
Trees depend on nutrients, such as magnesium and calcium, for their survival. In areas with high amounts of acid in the soil, often caused by acid rain, these nutrients are washed away and aluminium is produced which may be taken up by the roots. Then, the trees may literally starve to death.

Killing Europe's forests

OVER HALF of West Germany's great forests, including the famous Black Forest, are thought to be dead or dying because of acid rain damage and the future looks even bleaker. Some scientists reckon almost all of that country's forests could be dead by early next century. Elsewhere in Europe, the situation is also depressingly bad. In Switzerland a third of the forests are dying, almost a half of Holland's forests are showing signs of damage and two million acres of trees are dying in Czechoslovakia. So far, Britain has escaped the worst but it could be our turn next.

Right: Looking like some weird set in a sci-fi film, this burnt and twisted tree shows the devastating effect of acid rain in West Germany's Black Forest region.
Inset: Many priceless features of historic buildings are being destroyed by acid rain. At St Paul's Cathedral in London, some stonework is being eaten away at the rate of almost 3 cm every 100 years.

Power from the wind

WIND-POWER isn't new. For centuries, traditional windmills harnessed it to drive machinery that ground wheat into flour or pumped water. Today, modern versions of windmills, called wind turbines, are used to create electricity. Experimental turbines, up to 90 m high, are being tested in Britain and wind-power could provide 10 per cent of the country's energy needs by the year 2000. To replace a 600 megawatt oil-fired power station, a 'wind-farm' would need nearly 500 of these turbines and cover about 10 square miles. Even so, they could be built offshore and wind-power *is* a relatively cheap, clean and promising 'alternative' energy. Other 'alternatives' are water (hydro-electric), wave, tidal power and even heat from the hot rocks at the centre of the earth.

A row of wind turbines on a 'farm' in California, USA.

Power from the sun

SCIENTISTS are now looking at 'renewable' energy sources like the sun, which are safer, cleaner and won't run out. In theory, the sun could produce the world's energy requirements for a year in just half an hour! Solar power is already being used successfully in many parts of the world for heating domestic buildings and water.

To produce electricity on a grander scale, some scientists have even suggested building solar power stations in space where the sun shines all the time – solar cells already power most satellites in space. But, at present, solar power is too expensive and inefficient to produce *large* quantities of electricity commercially.

This solar power station has been built in the Pyrenees in southern Europe.

The nuclear debate

COAL, GAS AND OIL will eventually run out and other 'renewable' energy sources have their limitations. So, scientists have looked to nuclear energy which could provide all our needs. To some people, it's the future; to others, it's a world threat. Nuclear energy can be released by a process called *nuclear fission* which is when unstable atoms that make up things like uranium are split. A chain-reaction occurs which produces enormous amounts of power. In a nuclear reactor, this is controlled to make electricity, but in an atomic bomb it is uncontrolled and causes terrifying destruction. Scientists have also been able to recreate a process called *nuclear fusion* which is what produces the incredible energy that causes the sun and stars to shine. But so far they've only harnessed it for destruction, in the deadly hydrogen bomb. Fusion energy has yet to be tamed to produce electricity.

The case *for* . . .

Dounreay Nuclear Power Station, in Scotland. One of 400 reactors in 36 countries all over the world that are producing electricity.

Nuclear weapons such as Cruise missiles have great destructive power but supporters say they've helped keep the peace in Europe and prevented a Third World War.

SUPPORTERS OF *nuclear weapons* believe that the fear that they could be used has prevented another major world war, like the Second World War. That war ended when two 'atomic' bombs were dropped by America on the Japanese cities of Hiroshima and Nagasaki in 1945, killing more than 200 000 people and causing widespread destruction.

Supporters of *nuclear-generated electricity* argue that it is a relatively clean, safe, efficient way of making electricity. They say it causes less damage to the environment than burning fossil fuels; that more people die from air pollution caused by coal than from nuclear accidents or the small amounts of potentially dangerous radioactive waste produced by nuclear fission; and that only a tiny amount of raw uranium, compared to huge quantities of coal, is needed to produce the same amount of electricity. Nuclear power provides about 20% of Britain's electricity, and about 70% in France.

✔ YES to Nuclear!

★ Nuclear weapons may have prevented a world war.
★ Nuclear power doesn't cause damaging acid rain, deadly air pollution or the greenhouse effect.
★ Nuclear power stations are relatively safe.
★ Nuclear power stations safeguard fossil fuel resources which will, one day, run out.
★ Nuclear power produces relatively small amounts of dangerous high-level radioactive waste which is stored safely.
★ Nuclear fusion *could* meet all our future energy needs.

ACTION

● **_Find out_** more about nuclear power from involved organisations. (See page 63.)
● **_Discuss_** the issue with your family and friends.
● **_Persuade_** your teachers to organise projects about the subject.
● **_Organise_** debates about nuclear power, at school.
● **_Make your decision_**, knowing all the facts! You might support *nuclear-generated electricity* and be against *nuclear weapons* or vice versa. Alternatively, you might decide you're either 'for' or 'against' BOTH uses of nuclear energy.

An anti-nuclear war demonstration in Britain, in 1989, held by the CND as part of its worldwide campaign for nuclear disarmament.

✗ NO to Nuclear!

★ Nuclear weapons could destroy the world.
★ Nuclear weapon tests increase the amount of radiation in the atmosphere.
★ Nuclear power produces high-level radioactive waste which can be dangerous for thousands of years.
★ The safe storage of high-level waste can't be absolutely guaranteed.
★ Nuclear power produces other low- and medium-level radioactive wastes and discharges which have increased radioactivity in the sea.
★ Nuclear power station accidents have killed and severely injured people.

The case *against* . . .

A rare glimpse of the destruction caused by the nuclear disaster at Chernobyl in the Soviet Union, in 1986.

CAMPAIGNERS AGAINST *nuclear weapons* are horrified that we have created weapons, capable of destroying the world, in the name of 'peace'. In the 1960s they formed a protest organisation called The Campaign for Nuclear Disarmament (CND) which has been fighting ever since under the banner 'Ban the Bomb'. Campaigners against *nuclear-generated electricity* are worried about the potentially dangerous radioactive waste produced by nuclear power stations and the risk of accidents. They argue that high-level radioactive waste remains a threat to people for hundreds, possibly thousands, of years so safe storage can't be guaranteed. They also argue that the accidents at Three Mile Island in America, in 1979, and Chernobyl in the Soviet Union, in 1986, prove that nuclear power isn't as safe as is claimed. At Chernobyl, 30 people died, nearly 250 people suffered severe radiation injury and 135 000 people had to be evacuated from their homes.

'O ZONE FRIENDLY!' scream the spray cans from the supermarket shelves. Aerosol makers have been falling over themselves to go green – but do not be fooled. With or without CFCs, aerosols are not good for our planet. Most people have heard of chlorofluorocarbons – CFCs, for short. They are gases which are used to push out whatever is inside an aerosol. A few years ago, whether your can contained hairspray or floor polish, it also contained CFCs. CFCs are thought to be mainly responsible for destroying the ozone layer. Once governments were finally persuaded to accept that, they signed an agreement to cut down on CFCs in aerosols. But the ozone layer is far from saved – and it's up to us to act now!

Down with CFCs!

The ozone layer

O ZONE IS A GAS – poisonous if you breathe much of it in. Fifteen to 30 miles above the earth it protects us, absorbing harmful ultra-violet rays from the sun. The term 'ozone layer' is misleading because there isn't one. Ozone is spread across a broad band of the stratosphere, consisting of a mixture of gases. Ozone is only a small part of the mixture, but without it, there would probably be no life on earth.

In 1985, British Antarctic Survey scientists discovered that a giant hole had suddenly appeared in the ozone layer above the frozen southern continent. The size of the hole changes from year to year, but there is no doubt that the ozone layer is being destroyed.

In 1989, more worrying news came from the North Pole. There is an ozone hole in the Arctic, too. CFCs must be banned, totally, NOW. Even that won't stop the ozone destruction for 100 years – that's how long CFCs stay around in the atmosphere.

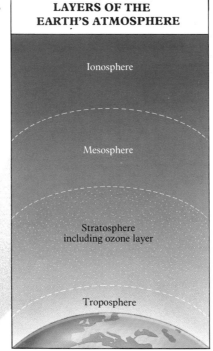

LAYERS OF THE EARTH'S ATMOSPHERE

Ionosphere

Mesosphere

Stratosphere including ozone layer

Troposphere

Instruments on weather balloons first alerted scientists to the hole in the ozone layer.

Ultra-violet alert!

A S OZONE IS DESTROYED, more of the sun's ultra-violet rays will get through to us. That will cause many more cases of skin cancer, especially in hot countries with light-skinned people, like Australia. People who sunbathe a lot will also be at risk. Untold damage may be done to plankton – the microscopic life in the oceans – which is destroyed by ultra-violet rays. Plankton is a vital link in the food chain and produces oxygen.

It is only recently that people have realised that too much sunbathing can be harmful to our skin.

CFC timebomb

RICH COUNTRIES are cutting back the amount of CFCs made. In poorer countries, like China and India, people are only now buying items like fridges and air conditioners that contain lots of CFCs. Hundreds of millions of Chinese want fridges, so the CFC problem could get much worse. An international treaty is needed, so rich countries provide the poorer ones with new chemicals that work as well as CFCs, but which do not damage the ozone layer.

Left: Fridges are new to most homes in China – the CFCs in them will have a big impact on the ozone layer.

The aerosol junkie

THERE'S A BLUE PETER PRESENTER who's probably responsible for a chunk of the hole in the ozone layer, and her name is Caron Keating!

Caron is a hairspray junkie. Presenters and producers have fled in terror just before the start of Blue Peter, when she really unleashes the stuff. At one time, she was using a big can a week! Fortunately, Caron, like millions of the rest of us, has learned the error of her ways. Now she uses only *pump-action* hairspray.

Due to pressure from shoppers, most stores now stock a large range of ozone-friendly sprays that do not have CFCs in them. But beware – there are still many sprays on the market which *do* contain CFCs.

And don't forget – NO aerosols are better than ozone-friendly aerosols. Even without CFCs, sprays may include harmful chemicals. Spray cans cannot be recycled and they are difficult to dispose of.

Left: When Caron sorted out so-called 'ozone-friendly' aerosols from the rest, she found that they were by far the larger group (the aerosols on Caron's right). Ozone-friendly or not, only a few of the sprays were pump action.

ACTION
- *Never* buy a spray with CFCs in it. Check the can.
- *Check packaging*. Fast-food might come in CFC 'blown' foam.
- *New fridges* can be bought with less CFCs in them. Old ones must be disposed of carefully. The CFCs can be drained out and recycled. Never dump an old fridge.
- *Cut back* on spray cans anyway. Do you really need them, or will something else do the job just as well?

Feeling like a swim?

W E CALL OUR PLANET, the Earth but oceans cover more than two-thirds of it and they are as important to our survival as land is. They are full of plants and animal life – everything from tiny single-celled organisms to the giant blue whale, the world's largest mammal. Just as we're destroying our countryside and endangering the animals there, we're also poisoning our seas and threatening the creatures that depend on them.

Oil pollution

P OLLUTION OF OUR oceans is difficult to see and, too often, it's a case of 'out of sight, out of mind'. But oil disasters show just how damaging it can be. One of the worst ever 'spills' happened in March 1989 when the giant supertanker the *Exxon Valdez*, carrying 53 million gallons of crude oil, went aground in Prince William Sound in Alaska. More than 10 million gallons of oil poured into one of the world's most beautiful waterways, polluting 2400 miles of natural, unspoiled coastline. Scientists *know* that the oil killed millions of fish, more than 30 000 birds and thousands of other wild creatures, including nearly 1000 sea otters. What they *don't know* is how many *more* animals died, but some people reckon that eventually up to three million birds could die because of this ONE oil disaster.

Far right: Workers face an almost impossible task as they try to clean up Alaska's beaches following the dreadful Exxon oil disaster, in 1989, which polluted thousands of miles of coastline. Inset: An oil-covered wild otter is caged, ready to send to a special cleaning centre. He probably survived but millions of other creatures died because of the pollution.

Poisoning our seas

THE WORLD'S OCEANS are used as giant dumping grounds for toxic chemicals, sewage sludge and radioactive waste. But this poisonous 'cocktail' is now threatening humans and wildlife. The Mediterranean and North Sea are both badly affected because huge amounts of pollution flow into them from the industrial areas of Europe. In 1987, an international conference agreed to try and clean up the North Sea by ending the dumping of harmful industrial waste there, by 1990, and cutting the amount of dangerous substances put into rivers and estuaries by half, by 1995.

Above: Children play around a waste pipe on Hastings beach. Left: Polluting our seas, as raw sewage is pumped out of an underwater pipe.

Bathers beware!

ONE IN THREE bathing beaches in England, Wales and Northern Ireland are officially designated as dirty and unsafe because the sewage in the water exceeds the standards set by the European community. Many of the pipes which discharge raw sewage into the sea aren't long enough to stop the waste returning to the shore. But, the Government hopes to have completely replaced or extended short pipes by 1995.

A grim warning for swimmers at the Farlington Nature Reserve in Hampshire.

Smothered by tiny plants

ALGAE IS IMPORTANT to our environment in the right quantities. But many rivers, lakes and coastal areas of Europe are now being smothered by damaging large-scale 'blooms' of algae. Certain weather conditions can produce them but they are also caused by too much nitrogen and phosphorus from fertilisers draining into water from farmland. When 'blooms' occur near fish farms they can suffocate and kill the fish. Some 'blooms' are also toxic and can poison shellfish and other creatures. In 1989 huge areas of the Italian Adriatic sea were polluted in this way, losing the country's tourism and fishing industries about 800 million pounds. So, *they* ended up paying for a problem caused by the agriculture and chemical industries!

Swimmers may be banned but a determined canoeist braves the polluted sea, carpeted with a thick algae 'bloom', off an Italian beach.

ACTION

Our world depends on the oceans for survival!

- ● *Look out* for pollution on the beaches and report it to the local council.
- ● *Don't* dump litter in the sea, in rivers or on beaches.
- ● *Find out* if water is clean before you go swimming in it.
- ● *Join* an organisation that's campaigning for cleaner rivers and seas (see page 63).

Sealife in danger

MANY OF THE world's sea creatures like seals, whales, dolphins, and porpoises are under threat of extinction because of the way we are treating them and their homes, the oceans. We are killing the animals by fishing and hunting, and 'drowning' the seas with poisonous chemicals. Scientists from the Greenpeace environmental organisation warn that if Europe's governments don't act NOW then dolphins and porpoises could disappear from the Baltic and North Sea, by the year 2000.

Saving our seals

IN 1988, 17 000 seals in the North Sea were killed by a *seal virus* similar to distemper which affects dogs. More than half the common seals on the east coast of Britain may have died in the epidemic which spread from the heavily polluted Baltic Sea. Rescue centres were set up around the country where sick seals were treated and, whenever possible, released back into the wild. There are big worries that pollution *might* be weakening the resistance of mammals to disease. Mammals *can* be badly affected by high levels of dangerous pollutants and the Government has begun major research into the problem. Chemicals like polychlorinated biphenyls (PCBs), used in generators and other industrial products, are a big threat. They get into the atmosphere and enter the seas, polluting small fish which are then eaten by other creatures in a 'food chain', ending with mammals at the top. The PCBs don't break down easily and are stored in the animals' fat. There is a world ban on the *production* of PCBs but Professor Joseph Cummins, from the University of Western Ontario in Canada, says that if the PCBs still *in use* aren't destroyed safely but get into the oceans instead then they could wipe out most, if not all, wild sea mammals, including seals.

Right: A healthy three-day-old grey seal pup in the Orkneys, off the north coast of Scotland. Inset: A sick common seal gets help at a special treatment centre following the outbreak of the seal virus in 1988.

Whales–Hunted to the brink

WHALES HAVE BEEN hunted, for food and other products, for thousands of years. But it wasn't until the 1870s that the mass slaughter of whales began, eventually threatening their existence. The invention of the grenade harpoon and the introduction of fast catcher boats, armed with bow-mounted cannons, meant whalers had much more efficient 'killing machines'. Now, even the giant blue whale, weighing up to 180 tonnes and 31 m long, fell victim. Each blue whale produced up to 30 tonnes of oil and so quickly became the main target. In 1930, the peak year, 30 000 of these magnificent creatures were killed. Today, it's *estimated* that there are fewer than 1000 'blues' left in the southern hemisphere, against nearly a quarter of a million before large-scale whaling began. Hunting is now officially banned. Only Japan and Norway still kill whales, mainly fin, sperm and minke, for what they call 'scientific' purposes!

Sperm whales under attack from whalers in 1868.

A flimsy Greenpeace inflatable boat challenges the might of a modern-day whaling ship in a protest against the slaughter of whales.

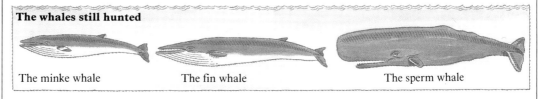

The whales still hunted

The minke whale   The fin whale   The sperm whale

Dolphins in danger

DOLPHINS, which have developed a special 'friendship' with humans over the centuries, are also threatened by pollution and people. Thousands of dolphins are dying around Japan's coasts as hunters cash in on the shortage of whale meat caused by the whaling ban. At least 130 000 more dolphins die each year by drowning when they get caught in tuna fishermen's nets. In parts of the eastern Pacific Ocean, the number of spinner dolphins has fallen by more than 80% since 1959. Greenpeace says only *urgent* action will save dolphins from extinction.

A bottle-nosed dolphin teaches a diver an underwater trick or two in the West Indies.

ACTION

Animals can't speak. You can. Be their voice!

● *Don't* dump litter in the sea, in rivers or on beaches.
● *Report* immediately to the police, coastguard or lifeguard, if you discover any animal stranded or washed up on the beach.
● *Look out* for wild mammals, off the coast, when you go on holiday.
● *Visit* a well-run marine park to find out more about the world's magnificent sea creatures.
● *Join* an organisation that's campaigning for cleaner seas and endangered sealife (see page 63).

A day at the coast

OVER 2000 miles of Britain's coast have already been lost under factories, roads, houses and shopping centres, and the remaining habitats of millions of rare birds, plants and seals are under threat. In 1965 the National Trust launched an appeal to save the last 900 miles of unspoilt coast from developers. It was called Enterprise Neptune and since then, through the efforts of campaigners and fundraisers, the scheme has been so successful that the National Trust recently celebrated its 500th mile of protected coast. The Trust doesn't just want to *preserve* the cliffs and beaches – it wants everyone to be able to enjoy a day at the coast. That means careful planning so people and wildlife can use the coast together.

Godrevy Point near Hayle in Cornwall.

Most people respect the coast and want to avoid causing damage. Signs are important because they tell people how to take care during their visits.

The Coastal Guardians

GODREVY POINT near Hayle in Cornwall is one of the National Trust's most beautiful stretches of coast and in the hot summer of 1989 it had over 100 000 visitors. One hundred thousand pairs of trampling feet caused a lot of damage to the walls and footpaths and, by the end of the holiday season, urgent repairs were needed. Godrevy's warden,

Ralph Calvert, couldn't cope on his own so he enlisted the help of some young volunteers – the Coastal Guardians!

The Coastal Guardians are all pupils of the Connors Down Primary School and they've made it their job to look after their local stretch of coast as John found out when he paid them a visit.

After the summer, many footpaths are badly worn and the grass needs time to grow again. The Coastal Guardians inspect the paths and note areas to be fenced off until the following year. Sand dunes are particularly at risk from erosion – when the grass is worn down the wind blows the sand away destroying the dunes.

The dry-stone walls at Godrevy are hundreds of years old and keep grazing cattle off the ancient heathland. When people take short cuts over walls the stones loosen until parts of the wall collapse. Ralph teaches the Coastal Guardians to repair walls in the traditional Cornish way.

ACTION

● **_When visiting_** the coast or National Parks, keep to the marked footpaths. They are the safest routes and help keep people off areas which are easily eroded.

● **_Never disturb_** nesting birds in spring and summer. If you enjoy catching seashore animals in rockpools, always put them back where you find them.

● **_If you spot_** hazardous rubbish on the beach, remove it if you can or inform the warden (on National Trust beaches) or the local council.

● **_Set up_** a group of volunteers like the Coastal Guardians to look after an area of coast or countryside you regularly visit.

Striking a balance

NOT ONLY THE the coasts are damaged by large numbers of visitors. Inland, thousands of people flock to the crags and moorlands of the Peak District and to the mountains of Snowdonia and the Lake District. Erosion is an enormous problem. Unless people stick to the footpaths, they gradually destroy the very thing they go there to enjoy. Preserving these areas is the work of the National Parks or the National Trust.

The Coastal Guardians patrol the beaches clearing up rubbish and debris. Washed-up chemical drums are treated with great care. The children first look for any danger signs, then check that the container is empty before taking it away.

Broken bottles and other rubbish left by holidaymakers are collected up. Occasionally, debris from shipwrecks is washed up and they report it to the Coast Guard.

Thousands of tourists have reduced this beauty spot in the Yorkshire Dales to a desert of scree.

Going fishing?

GO FISHING IN many of Britain's rivers and all you are likely to catch is a waterborne disease! When water gets polluted, fish are the first to die. Pollution upsets the whole balance of nature in our rivers and lakes, killing wildlife and spreading disease, sometimes in the most unlikely ways. In one incident, water drawn into a power station was so polluted that a mist of bacteria was sprayed over nearby villages from the cooling towers.

Most drinking water in Britain comes from rivers and reservoirs and goes to a water-treatment works to be purified before being pumped to our homes. The water-treatment works can only cope with certain levels of pollution so, if the water contains too many chemicals, they end up in our drinking water. No one knows how this affects our health.

All life on earth depends on water, yet we look after our water very badly. When it rains, more filth is washed into our rivers.

Below: Most tap water we use originally came from streams, reservoirs and rivers. This picture shows the many ways water can be polluted by the time it reaches our homes.

Industrial waste

Factories are often built alongside rivers so that liquid waste can be drained off into the water. Cancer-causing chemicals, such as benzene and toluene, are discharged into the River Mersey, and waste from one chemical plant on the River Tees contains cyanide, mercury and copper. Although there are laws about releasing these poisons into rivers, many factories escape prosecution because of legal loopholes.

Nitrates and phosphates

As water meanders downstream it gathers chemicals which seep into it from the land. Pesticides, and nitrate and phosphate fertilisers from farmland get into rivers and have devastating effects on wildlife. In areas of intensive farming, these chemicals can even end up in tap water.

Farm effluents

Factory-farming of pigs, cattle and poultry produces large quantities of manure which is usually sprayed onto fields. When this 'slurry' leaks into streams and rivers it causes 'blooms' of algae and bacteria which make the oxygen levels in water drop. This kills fish and other animals.

Landfill sites

Dangerous solvents and metals, such as cadmium and mercury from batteries, are buried in landfill sites. They seep through the soil and eventually find their way into rivers. Rubbish is not sorted before it is buried and so nobody knows exactly what these tips contain.

Accidental spillage

With so many factories built by rivers and an increasing number of chemical tankers on the roads, there are bound to be accidental spills. Other accidents can happen too: workmen misreading the dosage of a weedkiller killed wildlife in a West Midlands lake, and a fire at a glue factory in Warwickshire caused catastrophic river pollution.

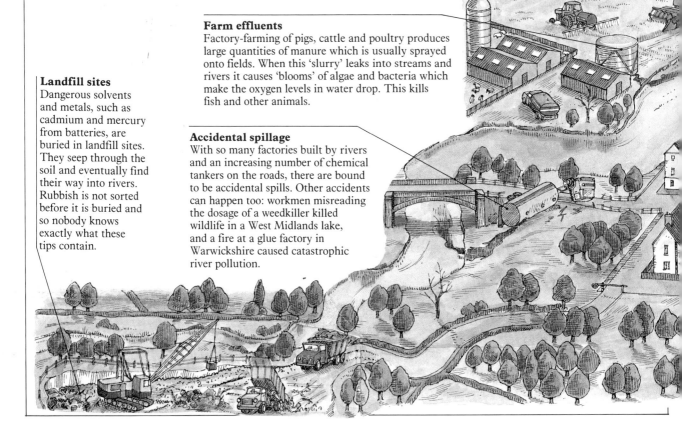

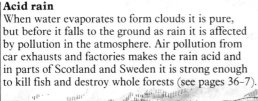

Acid rain

When water evaporates to form clouds it is pure, but before it falls to the ground as rain it is affected by pollution in the atmosphere. Air pollution from car exhausts and factories makes the rain acid and in parts of Scotland and Sweden it is strong enough to kill fish and destroy whole forests (see pages 36–7).

Sewage treatment

Waste water from our homes goes to the sewage works to be cleaned before being discharged back into the rivers. Organic matter is digested by bacteria in filter beds, but if the water contains chemicals, such as bleach, it kills the helpful bacteria. With ever-increasing volumes of water being pushed through old-fashioned sewage works, the system can't cope and in many areas polluted water gushes back into the river.

Household waste

When we pull the plug out of the kitchen sink we may be unleashing an army of chemicals into the sewage system. Washing-up water gets mixed with washing powders, toilet cleaners, shampoos, and paintbrush cleaners, to name but a few. It all puts a tremendous strain on the sewage works.

Is your river healthy?

SWANS ARE indicators of the health of our rivers and lakes. They can put up with a lot of human activity, even nesting where rubbish has been tipped into the water. But they can only tolerate a certain amount of pollution. Even in rural Stratford-upon-Avon the number of swans has dwindled from 100 pairs to just a few dozen. When the swans leave, what chance is there for other kinds of wildlife?

Mute swans nesting among the rubbish on an urban lake.

ACTION

● *Avoid* wasting water. Always turn off taps, and don't overfill baths. Cut down on the amount of water you use at home in any way you can. The more we use, the more need there will be to flood land with reservoirs.

● *Be careful* what you pour down the sink or toilet. Try to find 'environment-friendly' alternatives.

● *Keep* a 'pollution watch' on streams in your area. You just need a net, a white tray and a magnifying glass. Freshwater animals are the best indicators of clean water. Scoop up animals from under stones and weed and examine them: the greater the variety, the cleaner the water.

Creatures to look out for on your 'pollution watch'.

All these creatures live in clean water. But only the sludge worm, bloodworm and rat-tailed maggot also live in dirty water.

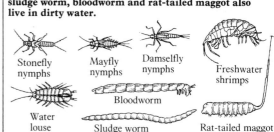

Stonefly nymphs | Mayfly nymphs | Damselfly nymphs | Freshwater shrimps

Water louse | Bloodworm | Sludge worm | Rat-tailed maggot

● *Report* polluted streams to the National Rivers Authority or your local Environmental Health Officer.

Animals matter

MORE THAN 200 SPECIES of mammals and birds have disappeared from the earth during the last 200 years. Today, hundreds more are fighting a battle for survival in an increasingly hostile world. Prince Philip, President of the World Wide Fund for Nature, has said that the death of a species is like 'the destruction of a unique work of art'.

Everywhere, animals are threatened. On the Savanna plains of Africa, the elephant is being ruthlessly killed for its ivory tusks and the endangered black rhino is being poached for its horns. In the mountain forests of China, the giant panda is facing extinction, as its traditional feeding grounds are destroyed. In the United States, the Californian condor is extinct in the wild and only survives in zoos. Meanwhile, in South America the destruction of unexplored rainforests could be killing off species of animals we don't even know exist!

Britain's wildlife is threatened too. Golden eagles are in danger because their traditional forests, home to the wildlife on which they prey, are disappearing. Bats, barn owls, red squirrels, natterjack toads and the common dormouse are just a few of the creatures facing extinction here. Their future is in *our* hands.

Extinct

THE DODO BIRD is one of the best-known creatures to have become extinct, as a result of us, in the last few hundred years. Bigger than a turkey, with blue-grey plumage, a big head and small useless wings, it was last seen in 1681. But many other animals have been wiped out too including: the South African quagga, a yellowish-brown zebra; the blue buck, a bluish-grey antelope; the Balinese tiger, the smallest of the 'big' cats; the Manchurian tiger; the Caspian tiger; the Caribbean monk seal and, sadly, many many more . . .

The dodo

Almost extinct

The Giant Panda
It's China's national symbol, the best loved of all wild creatures and one of the rarest. Hunting, which is forbidden now, and the destruction of their misty bamboo forests have pushed this cuddly-looking 'bear' close to extinction – fewer than a thousand remain in the wild. A huge campaign has been launched to save it.

The Common Dormouse
This bright orange creature with a bushy tail used to be common throughout Britain. But it's vanished from seven counties in the last 100 years and is now officially endangered. The threat to this tiny animal which eats fruit, seeds, buds and nuts has come from the destruction of its woodland home.

The Grey Wolf
It's the largest of the dog family and was once the most widespread mammal, apart from us, in Europe. Now it's only found in Eastern Europe, the Mediterranean region, the Middle East, Asia and North America. It's under threat from destruction of its habitat and farmers who kill it to protect their animals.

Battle to save the Black Rhino

THE RHINOCEROS, with its bare, leathery skin and grotesque appearance conjures up images of the huge reptilian dinosaurs that used to rule the world hundreds of millions of years ago. While the rhino is no reptile, it certainly *is* a relic from the past – rhinos were around up to 40 million years ago and, just like the dinosaurs, it's threatened with extinction.

Most at risk is Africa's black rhino. In 1970 there were more than 65 000. Today there are just 3500 left, half of them in Zimbabwe where *Blue Peter* went on its Summer Expedition in 1989. John and Yvette reported on the battle against Zimbabwe's poachers to save this endangered animal. The poachers are killing black rhinos for their horns at the rate of one a day. Each horn is worth up to £50 000 and they are used to make handles for daggers in the Middle East or traditional 'medicines'. It's an evil trade which is wiping out the black rhino.

John with endangered black rhino (left). John and warden with hundreds of rhino skulls (above).

Fighting for the African Elephant

THE AFRICAN ELEPHANT, the largest creature still walking the earth, is also being hunted to extinction. Poachers kill it for its valuable ivory tusks which are then turned into things like jewellery, chess sets and sculptures (often of elephants). The main market for these things is the Middle East and Far Eastern countries like Japan.

Between 1979 and 1989 an estimated 70 000 African elephants a year were slaughtered. If that continues, then the 625 000 elephants now left would be extinct in the wild by the year 2000. Some countries, like Kenya and Tanzania, have been worse hit than others. In Zimbabwe, as John and Yvette discovered, the elephant population actually grew from 30 000 to more than 40 000 during the same period. But the poachers stop at nothing and it could be Southern Africa's turn next.

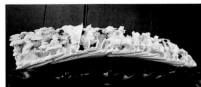

A herd of African elephants in the wild (top). An intricately carved elephant tusk (above).

ACTION

Animals CAN'T speak, we CAN. Be their voice! We must
- *Protect* all wild animals. Even if they're not endangered today, they could be tomorrow.
- *Fight* to stop the hunting of animals at home and abroad.
- *Preserve* the traditional habitats where wild animals live.
- *Never* buy jewellery, trinkets or souvenirs made from elephant ivory or rhino tusks.
- *Campaign* to stop the international ivory trade.
- *Join* wildlife organisations battling to save threatened animals (see p. 63).

THOUSANDS OF SPECIES of animals have been lost from the world for ever and nothing can bring *them* back. But *today's* endangered creatures, threatened mainly by the destruction of their wild habitat and hunting, *can* be saved by turning back nature's clock. By creating protected areas of wilderness and protecting the animals themselves, we can give them a better chance of survival. There are plenty of examples to show it works. One of the most successful campaigns to save an endangered species is 'Operation Tiger' which has brought the biggest of the 'big' cats back from the brink of extinction. Closer to home, there has been some success in the campaign to reintroduce the rare otter to our rivers and the magnificent osprey to our skies. Protected by us, all these creatures now have a safer future.

Back from the brink

The decline of the Tiger

Four British hunters and their helpers pose for a camera 'shoot' after killing three tigers in the Sirohi hills in India, in 1893.

THE TIGER, a fearful but magnificent creature, is one of the world's most successful *hunters*. It often kills animals much bigger than itself, sometimes even humans. But it's also been one of the most *hunted* by people. They killed the animal for 'sport' and for its valuable skin.

In 1900 there were about 100 000 tigers in Asia but by 1970, the year shooting them was banned, there were just 5000 left. They'd been hunted almost to extinction.

CLAWING BACK
India's tiger population
1900 – 40 000 tigers
1972 – 2000 tigers
1983 – 4000 tigers
1989 – 5000 tigers (estimate)

'Operation Tiger'

IN 1973, with the tiger facing extinction, the World Wide Fund for Nature and the Indian government set up 'Operation Tiger' – a joint campaign to save this threatened creature. They created nine special reserves where the tigers could breed in safety. The first was at Ranthambhore, a scrubland which was turning to desert because the grass had been grazed away by cattle. At the time there were just 14 tigers left there. Twelve villages were closed down, 1000 people and 10 000 cattle moved out and the land was handed back to nature. Today, it's a very different place – lush and green, with grass tall enough for tigers to hide in. Now there are more than 40 of the animals roaming freely through the park. They've even taken over the ruined fifteenth-century fortress which gives Ranthambhore its name – it's almost hidden by vegetation in this new wilderness. Other wildlife has also thrived. There are many more deer, monkeys, and peacocks than before. But the people weren't forgotten. They got new villages away from the reserve, complete with temples, schools, and fresh water supplies. There are now 16 such reserves in India and, with our help, the tiger's future now looks much more secure.

An Indian tiger roams free again in Ranthambhore, India, following the success of 'Operation Tiger', which was set up in 1973.

The return of the Osprey

THE OSPREY, a famous bird of prey, became extinct in Britain, in 1908, once again because of people. The birds were shot and collectors stole their rare eggs. In 1954 a pair of ospreys from Scandinavia nested in Scotland and since then, the RSPB has battled to increase the number that breed there after spending the winter in West Africa. It builds artificial nests for them, away from people, and once the eggs have been laid it guards the main sites 24 hours a day. Its efforts seem to be paying off – between 50 and 60 pairs of ospreys now breed in the Scottish Highlands every year.

Right: A female osprey with two young chicks. Once extinct in Britain, these magnificent birds are again nesting and breeding in the Scottish Highlands.

The Otter swims back

THE OTTER, one of Britain's best-loved rare creatures, was, until recently, only found in a few parts of the country like mid-Wales, North Yorkshire, Northumberland, and Scotland. But it now faces a brighter future than 30 years ago. Then, there were fears it would disappear from *all* of our rivers – pesticides and hunting nearly wiped it out. Since then it's slowly come back, helped by people, its old enemy. Otters, bred in captivity at places like the Otter Trust at Earsham in Norfolk, have been released into the wild in East Anglia and the South West of England where they've bred successfully.

Right: A female otter with her cubs at the Otter Trust in Earsham, Norfolk.

ACTION

● **Animals CAN'T speak, we CAN. Be their voice! We must *protect* all wild animals. Even if they're not endangered today, they could be tomorrow.**
● ***Preserve* the traditional habitats where wild animals live.**
● ***Never* remove eggs from birds' nests.**
● ***Create* your own artificial nesting site, at home or at school, with a bird box!**
● ***Provide* food and water for wild animals in your garden, especially in winter.**
● ***Campaign* to stop chemical pollution, particularly of rivers.**
● ***Join* wildlife organisations battling to save threatened animals (see page 63).**

Beauty and...

FOR THOUSANDS of years, people have *used* animals, in all sorts of ways, to make themselves look more 'beautiful'. Often it has caused a great deal of suffering and now more and more people are saying that it's wrong to treat creatures in this way. Often, animals or parts of them are used as ingredients in make-up, for jewellery, fashion accessories or clothing. Animals are also used to test the huge variety of beauty products that people demand, everything from shampoos and soaps to lipsticks and perfumes. Whales, elephants, 'big' cats, exotic birds, dogs and rabbits are just a few of the many creatures that have fallen victim to people's desire to look more 'attractive'. It's been a high price for 'beauty', at a high cost to the 'beast'.

'Cruelty-free' beauty

A huge choice of 'cruelty-free' make-up products are now available in shops.

MANY SHOPS now stock a large range of good quality beauty products and toiletries, made without cruelty to animals, and there's a growing demand for them. In 1989, a MORI survey revealed that almost nine out of ten people were *against* products being tested on animals and the same number wanted clear labelling to show if items were 'cruelty-free'. Half of the people said they'd switch to other products if they found that the brands they were using had been tested on animals and most said they'd pay extra, if necessary. In the same year two of the top six major international cosmetic and toiletries firms stopped animal testing of their products.

....the beasts

Left: Half of Caron's face (on the left-hand page) was made-up with 'cruelty-free' cosmetics and the other half with products tested on animals. Can you tell the difference? Caron couldn't!

'Cruel' beauty

IN 1989, an estimated 14 000 animals were used in Britain for cosmetic and toiletries tests but that's a tiny number compared to the 70 million used in America for all reasons. One experiment, called the 'Draize' test, involves dropping concentrated products, such as new shampoos, into creatures' eyes to see if they are likely to cause eye irritation in humans. Sometimes this leads to blindness and even death. Many people say other scientific methods that don't exploit animals should be used to discover if products are safe.

A rabbit faces up to the Draize test – an experiment that involves dropping products into the creature's eyes to see if they're likely to cause irritation when used on people.

Animal fashion

RARE BIRDS have been killed and had their feathers plucked to grace people's hats and clothing. Mighty whales have been hunted close to extinction for their oil which was used, among other things, as a wax base for a wide variety of cosmetics like lipstick, rouge and eyeshadow. Endangered creatures, such as leopards, have been killed for their skins to make expensive coats. The number of animals that have been exploited is huge. Yet the international 'beauty' trade in threatened creatures and their products still goes on today!

The furs from at least *40* beautiful Geoffroy's cats (top) are needed to make just *1* fur coat for a person who wants to look more 'beautiful' (above).

Crocodiles (top) suffer dreadful cruelty when they're killed, at about four years old, for their skins that are made into things like handbags (above). Sometimes the animals are skinned alive because it's thought it produces a higher quality 'leather'.

ACTION

Animals can't talk. You can, be their voice!
- *Buy* 'cruelty-free' cosmetics and toiletries.
- *Ask* your local shop or supermarket to stock 'cruelty-free' products.
- *Don't buy* jewellery or fashion accessories made with products from endangered animals (see pages 50–1).
- *Don't buy* fur coats or jackets, made from the skins of endangered animals.
- *Join* an organisation campaigning to stop cruelty to animals (see page 63).

The Green

IT STARTED WITH the ozone-friendly aerosols. Suddenly, supermarkets are falling over themselves to be greener than each other. They have discovered that shoppers – that's *us* – will choose one item instead of another because it does less harm to our planet. Aerosols are just the beginning. Things are changing . . . all thanks to the birth of the GREEN SHOPPER! It is easy to make sure the family uses ozone-friendly sprays. But nobody should feel smug, if that is all they are doing. Just because you accept the 'better' product offered by the supermarkets does not automatically mean it is the best one for the environment.

Aerosols

ALL THE supermarkets now stock ozone-friendly sprays. But even ozone-friendly sprays are not really planet-friendly. They take a lot of energy to produce and are difficult to dispose of. Stick to pump-action sprays, and try and use fewer of them anyway. Rushing out and buying lots of ozone-friendly sprays in the mistaken belief that somehow they are good for the earth is quite wrong. They are just *less bad* than the old type.

Eggs

HEALTH SCARES about eggs in 1988 alerted people to the possible dangers involved in the way most of our eggs are produced. If you are concerned about the conditions that egg-laying hens live in, then buy free-range eggs. They must say 'free-range' on the box, and the box will almost certainly be cardboard. Avoid any eggs that come in plastic boxes, because of the problems of disposing of plastic.

Fruit and vegetables

NOT SO LONG AGO, if you were buying organically-grown fruit and vegetables, you were probably in a health-food shop. Now you could be in any of the big supermarkets. They have all started selling produce that has been grown without the use of chemical fertilisers or pesticides. The more people buy it, the cheaper it will get, the more will be available, and the healthier the soil in the countryside will become.

Nappies

AS ANYONE with a younger brother or sister will know, most families now use disposable nappies. They make the whole business much easier. But there are four big problems with them. First, trees have to be cut down and turned into pulp which makes the soft inside of each nappy. Second, to make the nappy look white, the pulp is bleached, possibly with chlorine which pollutes rivers. Third, a lot of each nappy is plastic, which is difficult to dispose of. Finally, used nappies take up a lot of space in landfill sites.

Some problems have been tackled. *In 1989, every major maker of nappies in Britain stopped using chlorine bleach to whiten nappies!*

That shows the power of the Green Shopper!

What can you use instead of disposables? Cloth nappies? They are less convenient and, if everyone used them and had to wash them, the cost to the environment would be enormous. Think of all the extra fossil fuels burned to make electricity and the extra washing powder flushed down the drain. Parents should use disposables, but choose ones that do less harm to the environment.

Phosphate and petro-chemical detergent-free goods include: washing-up liquids, washing powders, fabric conditioners, and other cleaning agents.

Goods include: stationery, toilet rolls and other goods made from recycled paper, mercury-free batteries, disposable nappies made using modified bleaching, pump-action aerosols, and PDCB-free toilet fresheners.

Organic foods include: wholemeal bread, rolls and flour, yoghurt, cheese, carob and banana drink, oats, coffee, free-range eggs, plus bleach-free coffee filters.

Organic fruit and vegetables include: grapefruit, oranges, pears, apples, lemons, carrots, cucumbers, green cabbage, red cabbage, lettuce, leeks, celery, red and green peppers, mushrooms, tomatoes, onions, garlic, turnips, and potatoes.

Shopper

Plastic bags

SUPERMARKETS love plastic bags! They love giving you half a dozen new ones free every time you shop! Unfortunately, plastic bags are not easy to dispose of. Once you throw them away, they do not break down in landfill rubbish sites. It's much better to buy a couple of sturdy shopping bags and use them again and again.

Packaging

LOTS OF THINGS we buy have far too much plastic, or paper, wrapped around them or they come inside glass or metal containers that are expensive to make or to move around once they're discarded. But we do need packaging – otherwise your baked beans would be in a puddle on the floor. People must try and cut down on things that are over-packaged (things that have two or more layers of packaging, like a box of chocolates). What you can recycle, should be recycled (see pages 20–1).

Batteries

MOST PEOPLE have a toy that works on batteries, and there are lots of things around the house that need them, like torches, clocks and personal stereos. Batteries often contain very small amounts of harmful substances, like mercury and cadmium. There are some available which contain little or no mercury – sometimes they claim to be 'green batteries', which is not quite true – all batteries do some harm to the environment.

Look for the Soil Association symbol on organic foods.

ACTION

- *Always* go for the 'greener' product if there is a choice.
- *Beware* of being fooled into thinking a 'greener' product is always the best thing for the planet.
- *Try* organic fruits and vegetables.
- *Buy* in bulk if possible. Buy family packs instead of lots of small items.
- *Choose* mercury-free batteries, but always use as few batteries as possible.
- *Reject* over-wrapped, needlessly packaged items.
- *Get* a sturdy shopping bag!

Graffiti's Here, OK?

THE *Oxford English Dictionary* defines graffiti as, 'A drawing or writing, scratched on a wall or other surface'. Taking this as a definition, people have been doing graffiti since the Stone Age when they etched drawings on cave walls. Today, it surrounds us and every school in Britain probably has some. Graffiti is everything from initials carved into desks to rude scribbling scratched onto toilet walls for everyone to see. Now the word graffiti is also used to describe drawings, slogans or words created in public places with marker pens or paint that's often sprayed from aerosols. Is it art or vandalism?

Graffiti as art

SOME MODERN-DAY graffiti can certainly be called art but which types are thought to enrich and improve our environment and which types aren't? *Most* people would probably say that graffiti is art when it's done in an *organised* way, for the enjoyment of those who are likely to see it, in things like murals. But a *few* people say that some *unorganised* graffiti, created for certain groups of people to enjoy, can also be called art. Exhibitions of 'unofficial' graffiti have been held at places like the South London Art Gallery in Peckham and books about graffiti 'street art' have also been published.

Top: Organised graffiti, at Laycock primary school in London, adds colour and interest to a dull and empty brick wall.
Above: A graffiti mural brings a bare wall to life at the Pepys housing estate in London.
Left: Unofficial graffiti 'piece'. Art or vandalism? The decision is yours!

Graffiti as vandalism

MOST GRAFFITI is done by people who are more interested in selfishly defacing our cities than improving them. The ugliest graffiti is called 'tagging' which is when people write their personal 'signature' in public areas, sometimes even on historic buildings, with markers or spray paint. 'Tagging' started in New York in America, in the 1970s but now it's spread to many European cities and London's Underground has become a big target. It's a crime and the 'taggers' face great dangers. Some have been killed by falling onto live railway lines. 'Tagging' sometimes frightens people and it's costing Britain hundreds of millions of pounds a year – money that could be used to improve our environment in other ways and make our country a more attractive place to live in.

ACTION

● *Tell* people it's illegal and selfish to do graffiti on public property without permission.
● *Persuade* people who want to do graffiti to get involved in organised murals or put their ideas on canvas.
● *Join* an organisation, like The Tidy Britain Group, that campaigns to clean up and stop ugly graffiti such as 'tags' (see page 63).

Above left: 'Tags' on a building in Amsterdam, Holland. Many European cities are now badly 'polluted' by this particularly ugly and selfish type of graffiti.
Above: This isn't 'art', it's pure vandalism.
Left: 'Tagging' trains is strictly illegal and extremely dangerous. It also upsets passengers and costs millions of pounds a year to remove.

Taking action

ALL OVER Britain young people are leading the way in persuading others to improve their surroundings. At Muswell Hill in London, a group of children got together and formed the first Junior Friends of the Earth which now has over 150 members. They are going to campaign to get supermarkets to give away durable bags instead of plastic ones, following a survey of the number of plastic carriers given away. They also plan to petition for a zebra crossing to make a local street safer for children. They campaign for change by setting a good example and then explaining to others what they are doing.

N Hill JUNIOR 🌍 Friends of the Earth

...e cleaning your street.

...an help solve the litter ...m.

...t drop litter yourself, tell others not to.

...all household rubbish ...gs and leave them

... your garden gate.

...t dump big items in ...treet, phone 8013026

...ection.

...o buy things...

Litter is a big problem, especially outside local fast-food restaurants, so the group has been campaigning to clean up the streets (above). Clearing rubbish in front of people makes passers-by think twice about dropping litter (above right). The group talks to shoppers about the problems of litter and gives out its anti-litter leaflets (left) which are printed on recycled paper.

Four thousand trees are consumed to produce just one day's worth of a daily newspaper. The group encourages people to recycle paper by collecting newspaper and taking it to the local recycling centre.

JUNIOR ... RECY...

SECOND-H... CLOTHES, B...

Putting an official tip next to Queen's Wood has encouraged illegal 'flytipping'. To gain support for their campaign to get dumping stopped, members show a Haringey local councillor the tangle of hazardous debris and illegally dumped waste which has piled up in the wood.

Campaign for your area

Where badgers once foraged and birds used to sing, six lanes of traffic now thunder. This ancient woodland in Surrey was sacrificed to build the M25 motorway.

Waste not, want not! Members hold a 'recycling sale' at the church hall (above). Items on sale include second-hand books, children's toys, and recycled writing paper and envelopes. Second-hand clothes are first cleaned, mended and ironed before being put on the stall. Their advert for the sale (below) is displayed in homes and shops.

Organically-grown vegetables are grown on the group's allotment (above). Some were available at the recycling sale which prompted many donations.

I F VANDALS destroy the stonework on an old building or damage trees in a wood, people want to take action. But this isn't the only form of 'vandalism' that takes place. Developers call factories 'business parks' now, but they still swallow up the countryside and so do new roads. The decision to build them is often taken by people who live miles away. It is important that local people should be involved in decisions which affect their own area. If you have strong views about a place near you that might be changed, set up or join a pressure group to put your ideas across. Thousands of people whose local area may be changed by the building of the Channel tunnel have done just this.

The Green *Blue Peter*

AS YOU READ this book, planet earth, and all the creatures who live on it, is under threat. But, it's not too late to save it and you – the children of today – will be the people who shape the future. By putting the tips in the Action Boxes into action you'll be playing an important part in changing the world for the better and you could also earn yourself a **Green *Blue Peter* Badge**! Since we launched the **Green *Blue Peter* Badge** on the programme in 1988, we've been flooded with letters, ideas, drawings and poems from children across Britain who care about the environment. The ones on these two pages are just a handful of the tens of thousands we've received on a huge variety of topics – if we'd published them all, we'd have filled several volumes of books! We know that this book will only be as helpful in saving our planet as the people who read it, so now it's up to YOU. Let us know what you think and what you're up to by writing to *Blue Peter*, BBC TV Centre, Wood Lane, London W12 7RJ and remember there's a **Green *Blue Peter* Badge** waiting for you!

Badge

Leave us alone

"ay

BYE"

The Year 2005

Aluminium Can Recycling Association (ACRA),
I-MEX House,
52, Blucher Street,
Birmingham B1.
Offers cash for used aluminium cans for recycling.

Beauty Without Cruelty International,
57, King Henry's Walk,
London N1 4NX.
Against animal experiments, especially in the process of making beauty products.

British Union for the Abolition of Vivisection (BUAV),
16a, Crane Grove,
Islington, London N7 8LB.
Against all animal experiments. Will send a free guide to cruelty-free products.

Campaign for Lead-Free Air (CLEAR),
3, Endsleigh Street,
London WC1H 0DD.
Campaigns against lead in petrol and other lead pollution.

Carnivorous Plant Society,
Mr & Mrs D. Watts,
174, Baldwins Lane,
Croxley Green,
Herts WD3 3LQ.
Provides advice on how to grow insect-eating plants.

Compassion in World Farming (CIWF),
20, Lavant Street,
Petersfield, Hants GU32 3EW.
Against the abuse of farm animals and wildlife.

Council for the Protection of Rural England (CPRE),
Warwick House,
25, Buckingham Palace Road,
London SW1W 0PP.
Campaigns to protect the countryside against development.

Department of Energy,
Thames House South,
Millbank, London SW1P 4QJ.
Government department responsible for energy.

Department of the Environment (DoE),
43, Marsham Street,
London SW1P 3PY.
Government department responsible for the environment.

Department of Transport,
2, Marsham Street,
London SW1P 3EB.
Government department responsible for transport.

Fauna and Flora Preservation Society (FFPS),
79–83, North Street,
Brighton BN1 1ZA.
Campaigns to protect areas with wild plants and flowers.

Friends of the Earth,
26–28, Underwood Street,
London N1 7JQ.
Campaigns to protect the environment.

Glass Manufacturers Federation,
Northumberland Road,
Sheffield,
Yorks S10 2UA.
Encourages the use and recycling of glass bottles.

Greenpeace,
30–31, Islington Green,
London N1 8XE.
Campaigns to protect the world's seas and the creatures in them.

Lynx,
PO Box 509,
Dunmow, Essex CM6 1UH.
Against the fur trade.

Men of the Trees,
Sandy Lane,
Crawley Down,
West Sussex RH10 4HS.
Campaigns to save trees and forests, worldwide.

National Anti-Vivisection Society (VAVS),
51, Harley Street,
London W1N 1DD.
Against animal experiments.

National Centre for Alternative Technology,
Llwyngwern Quarry,
Machynlleth,
Powys SY20 9AZ.
The centre is experimenting with 'alternative' energy, including wind power and solar energy.

National Trust,
36, Queen Anne's Gate,
London SW1H 9AS.
Protects and preserves Britain's countryside and historic buildings.

Nature Conservancy Council,
Northminster House,
Peterborough,
Cambs PE1 1UA.
Campaigns to protect Britain's countryside and wildlife.

Open Spaces Society,
25a, Bell Street,
Henley-on-Thames,
Oxon RG9 2BA.
Campaigns to protect common land and public footpaths.

Oxfam,
274, Banbury Road,
Oxford OX2 7DZ.
Recycles waste to raise money for the poor, worldwide.

Royal Society for the Prevention of Cruelty to Animals (RSPCA),
Causeway,
Horsham,
West Sussex RH12 1HG.
Campaigns to stop cruelty to animals.

The Soil Association Ltd,
86–88, Colston Street,
Bristol BS1 5BB.
Concerned with organic produce and gardening.

Tidy Britain Group,
The Pier,
Wigan,
Greater Manchester WN3 4EX.
Campaigns against litter.

Transport 2000,
Walkden House,
10, Melton Street,
London NW1 2EJ.
Campaigns for environment-friendly transport policies.

Watch,
c/o The Royal Society for Nature Conservation (RSNC),
22, The Green,
Nettleham,
Lincoln LN2 2NR.
Young people's conservation group that campaigns to protect the countryside and wildlife.

Whale and Dolphin Conservation Society,
20, West Lea Road,
Weston,
Bath BA1 3RL.
Campaigns to protect the world's whales and dolphins.

Woodland Trust,
Autumn Park,
Dysart Road,
Grantham,
Lincs NG31 6LL.
Campaigns to preserve woodlands.

World Society for the Protection of Animals,
106, Jermyn Street,
London SW1Y 6EE.
Works worldwide to protect all kinds of animal life.

Worldwide Fund for Nature UK (WWF),
Panda House,
Weyside Park,
Godalming,
Surrey GU7 1XR.
Campaigns to save endangered animals, worldwide.

Young Ornithologists Club (YOC),
c/o Royal Society for the Protection of Birds (RSPB),
The Lodge, Sandy,
Beds SG19 2DL.
Young people's organisation that campaigns to protect birds, worldwide.

Young People's Trust for the Environment and Nature Conservation,
95, Woodbridge Road,
Guildford,
Surrey GU1 4PY.
Young people's organisation that campaigns on conservation issues.

Index

Acid Rain, 6, 34–6, 38, 48
Aerosols, 19, 40–1, 56
Air Pollution, 6, 24, 32–8, 48
Aluminium, 21, 36
America, 14–16, 18, 38–9, 50, 59
Animals, 6, 8, 10–12, 14, 24, 26, 28, 31, 36, 44–5, 47–55, 63
Aphids, 11
Atmosphere, 15, 17–19, 33–4, 39–41, 44

Badgers, 8, 12, 61
Bats, 9, 50
Batteries, 33, 48, 57
Beaches, 46–7
Beetles, 8, 9, 28
Bicycles, 19, 24
Birds, 6, 8–9, 11, 14, 29–31, 46–7, 50, 52–5
Bleach, 21, 49, 56
Bottles, 7, 20–1, 25, 47
Butterflies, 8, 11

Carbon dioxide, 14, 18–19, 32, 40–1
Cars, 4, 6–7, 18–19, 32–5, 37, 48, 56
Cats, 26–7, 32, 50, 52, 54
Catalytic converters, 32–3, 35, 37
Caterpillars, 8, 9
Cattle, 8, 16, 19, 47–8, 52
Chlorofluorocarbons (CFCs), 16, 18, 40–1
Chemicals, 6, 10–11, 44, 48–9, 56
Chernobyl, 39
Chlorine, 21, 56
Climate, 14, 28
Coal, 7, 10, 19, 20, 34–5, 38, 41
Compost, 21, 25
Conifers, 12
Cosmetics, 54–5, 63
Countryside, 4, 8, 10–12, 24, 28, 47, 57, 61
Crops, 10–11, 14, 20
Cyanide, 48

Deserts, 12, 24
Dodo, 50
Dogs, 26–7, 44, 54
Dolphins, 44–5

Eggs, 8, 31, 52–3, 57
Electricity, 6–7, 19, 24–5, 34–5, 37–9, 41, 56

Elephants, 6, 15, 50–1, 54–5
Energy, 7, 18–20, 25, 33–41, 56

Farming, 8, 10–11, 14, 16, 48
Fast-food, 18, 40, 60
Fertilizers, 6, 10–11, 48, 56
Fish, 10, 17, 29, 34, 36, 44, 48
Flowers, 8, 12, 15, 20, 28
Food, 8–12, 14, 16–21, 24, 32, 39, 40–1, 44, 53
Footpaths, 31, 46–7
Forests, 6, 12, 14–17, 19, 36, 49–50
Fossil-fuels, 34
Fridges, 18, 40
Fruit, 56
Fuels, 4, 10, 19, 24, 25, 33, 34, 38, 41, 56, 63
Fur, 55, 63
Furniture, 15, 25

Gas, 10, 18–19, 34–5, 38, 40–1, 63
Glass, 4, 19, 20, 25, 41, 57
Goldsworthy, Andy, 22–3
Gorillas, 14
Graffiti, 24, 58–9
Grass, 22, 28, 46, 47, 52
Greenhouse effect, 18–19, 24–5, 32, 38, 40–1
Greenpeace, 44–5

Hamburgers, 16
Hardwoods, 25
Health-food, 56
Heat, 14, 18–20, 25–6, 35–7, 40–1
Hedgehogs, 9, 11
Hedgerow, 8, 9, 28
Hens, 7, 57
Hydrocarbons, 32
Hydrogen, 33, 35, 38
Hydro-electric, 37

Insects, 6, 9, 11–12, 15, 28
Ivory, 6, 50–1

Ladybirds, 11
Lakes, 6, 30–1, 34, 36, 48–9
Landfill sites, 19–20, 48, 56–7
Lead, 32–3
Leaves, 8–9, 22–3, 28
Leopards, 55
Litter, 4, 9, 17, 21, 45, 60
Lorries, 35

Macaw, 15
Mahogany, 15, 25
Make-up, 54–5
Mammals, 9, 11, 44, 45, 50

Meat, 16, 19, 41, 45
Medicines, 12, 14–15, 20, 51
Mercury, 48–9, 57
Metal, 19–21, 25, 32, 41, 49, 57
Methane, 18–19, 40–1
Monkeys, 52
Motorways, 12, 30, 32, 61

Nappies, 56
Neutering, 26
Nitrates, 10, 48
Nitrogen, 32, 35
Nuclear, 6, 34, 38, 39, 63

Oak, 12–13, 15, 28
Oil, 7, 19, 20, 34, 38, 41, 45, 55
Ospreys, 7, 52–3
Otters, 52, 53, 63
Owls, 50
Oxygen, 10, 14, 35, 48
Ozone, 16, 18, 40
Ozone-friendly, 56

Pacific Ocean, 45
Packaging, 16, 17, 24, 57
Panda, 50
Paper, 16, 20, 21, 25, 57, 60
Polychlorinated biphenyls (PCBs), 44
Perfumes, 54
Pesticides, 8, 10, 11, 48, 53, 56
Pests, 10–11
Pets, 15, 21, 26
Petrol, 10, 19, 32–3, 41, 56–7
    unleaded, 7, 32–3, 37
Phosphates, 48
Phosphate-free, 25
Plants, 6, 8–10, 14–15, 28–9, 31, 33, 36, 46
Plastic, 16, 18, 20–1, 25, 34, 40, 56–7, 60
Pollination, 9
Pollution, 6, 20, 24–5, 34–8, 44–5, 48–9, 53
Ponds, 28
Porpoises, 44
Potatoes, 17

Radioactivity, 38–9
Rainforests, 6, 14–17, 19, 25, 41, 50
Recycling, 4, 7, 20, 21, 24, 25, 26, 60
Reservoirs, 48–9
Rhinoceros, 50–1
Rivers, 4, 10, 20, 35–6, 45, 48–9, 52–3, 56
Roads, 15, 46, 48

Rockpools, 47
RSPB, 30–1, 52, 63
RSPCA, 26–7
Rubbish, 4, 6–7, 16, 18, 20–1, 24, 40, 47, 49, 56–7, 60

Schools, 21, 29, 32, 39, 46, 52–3, 58
Sea, 6, 18, 19, 34, 35, 39, 40, 41, 44, 45
Seals, 44, 46, 50
Sewage, 49
Shampoos, 49, 54–5
Slugs, 8–9, 11
Snails, 8–9, 11
Soil, 10, 11, 13–14, 16, 20, 28, 36, 49, 57
Solar, 33, 36–7
Soya, 16
Spiders, 9
Streams, 10, 18, 40, 48, 49
Sun, 14, 18, 33–4, 36–8, 40
Supermarkets, 10–11, 55–7, 61

Temperature, 18, 40
Thrush, 8, 9, 11, 29
Tigers, 50, 52
Toads, 11, 50
Topsoil, 8, 11, 28
Trains, 34, 58
Trees, 8–9, 12–16, 19–20, 28, 36, 41, 56, 60, 61
Typhoons, 18, 40

Uranium, 38

Vandalism, 24, 58, 61
Vegetables, 10, 11, 56, 57, 61
Vegetarians, 19, 41

Waste, 20–1, 24–5
    radioactive, 39
    water, 48–9
Wastepaper, 21
Water, 10, 12, 18–20, 28, 30, 35–7, 40–1, 48–9, 52–3
Weather, 18
    weather balloon, 40
Weedkiller, 48
Weeds, 10, 13
Whales, 44–5, 54–5
Wildlife, 4, 8, 10, 12, 14, 24–5, 28–9, 31, 35, 46, 48–53
Wind, 7, 37, 46
Wind-power, 37
Wood, 12, 15, 19, 25, 28, 61
Woodland, 9, 12, 25, 28, 36, 49
Worms, 9, 21, 30, 49

Picture credits (key: l – left, r – right, t – top, c – centre, b – bottom, tl – top left, tr – top right, cl – centre left, cr – centre right, ct – centre top, cb – centre bottom, bl – bottom left, br – bottom right)
Agence Rapho (H. Silvester), **p.6** (tl) & **15–16** (also on back cover); Alan Jacobs Gallery/Bridgeman Art Library, **p.12**; Barnaby's Picture Library, **p.43** (tl); Andrew Besley, **p.46** (t); British Coal, **p.34** (t); BUAV **p.55** (l); Bruce Coleman, **p.6** (br, M. Boulton), 7 (br, H. Reinhard), 8 (r, R. Wilmshurst), 18 (t, J. Foott), **36** (b, A. Davies), **37** (b, F. Sauer), **40** (r, D. Orchard), **51** (c, H. Reinhard, also on back cover), **52** (b, G. Ziesler), **53** (t, J. van Wormer), **55** (ct, L. C. Marigo; bc, H. Reinhard) & **61** (r, A. Davies); Colorific, **p.6** (tr, B. Eppridge), **34** (br), **39** (l, S. Benbow) & **50** (t, F. Fournier); Dr Horace Dobbs, **p.45** (b); Ecoscene, **p.7** (tr, Gryniewicz), **20** (l, S. Morgan), **37** (t, S. Morgan) & **43** (b, I. Harwood); Mary Evans Picture Library, **p.45** (t); Brian Goddard (for Cats' Protection League), **p.26** (bl); Andy Goldsworthy, **p.22** (b, J. Calder), **22–3** & **23** (all Fabian Carlsson Gallery); Sally & Richard Greenhill, **p.32** (t) & **59** (r); Greenpeace, **p.44** & **45** (c); Robert Harding, **p.12–13**, **18** (b), **27** (cr), **36–7**, **38** (l), **43** (cl), **51** (b), **58** (t & c) & **59** (l); Holt Studios (N. Cattlin), **p.17**; Hutchison Library, **p.41** (t, M. Friend); ICCE, **p.6** (cr, C. Rose), 7 (tl, J. Baines; bl, M. Boulton), **13** (t, P. Steele), **34** (bl, M. Tasker) & **55** (b, G. Shayle); India Office Library/British Library, **p.52** (l); London Zoo, **p.50** (b); Magnum, **p.42** (both P. Fusco); Muswell Hill Junior FOE, **p.61** (bl); NHPA, **p.13** (b, S. Dalton), **49** (M. Leach) & **52–3** (G. Lacz); Oxford Scientific Films, **p.8** (l, R. Toms), **14–15** (also on back cover), **44–5** (T. Martin) & **50** (l, M. Leach); Rex Features, **p.6** (bl, Novosti/Sipa), **33** (c, N. Jorgensen), **38** (r, Astral), **39** (r, Sipa), **40** (bl, Sipa/P. Dumas), **43** (r, G. de Bellis), **58** (b) & **59** (b); RSPB, **p.7** (cr, M. Richards), **30** & **31** (t, all C. Nicholson); Science Photo Library, front cover & **p.1** (globe); Today, **p.33** (t); Philip Wayre, **p.53** (b); Yorkshire Dales National Park, **p.47** (br). The following were taken for the BBC by: Andrew Besley, **p.46–7** (except br); Peter Brown, **p.29** (b) & **51** (t); Dave King, **front cover** & **p.20** (r), **20–1** (also on back cover), **41** (c) & **54**; Karl Shone, **p.5**, **10**, **27** (t & b), **31** (except t), **33** (b), **55** (tr), **56–7**, **60** & **61** (t & c); Dr Jane Smart, **p.28** & **29** (l & r). All remaining photographs are BBC copyright.
Illustrators: Steve Carey, Kuo Kang Chen, Richard Phipps, Jim Robbins & John Woodcock.